WRITERS in the LAKES

Alan Hankinson

BOOKCASE

Alan Hankinson

ISBN 978-1-904147-39-8
Published by Bookcase
19 Castle Street, Carlisle. CA3 8SY 01228 544560
www.bookscumbria.com
Printed and bound by CPI Antony Rowe, Eastbourne

INTRODUCTION

Alan Hankinson, known to all as 'Hank' died on 22nd March 2007. He had led a rich and varied life. He was born in Gately, Cheshire, in 1926, educated at Bolton School in Lancashire and won a scholarship to read modern history at Magdalen College, Oxford, graduating in 1949.

His university career was interrupted by war service, briefly with the Black Watch and then as an officer with the Royal Gurkha Rifles.

He became a journalist with the Bolton Evening News and a lifelong Bolton Wanderers' supporter and later became news editor at the Nigerian Broadcasting Corporation.

In 1958 he joined Independent Television News. In his three decades at ITN he filled many roles: as scriptwriter, programme editor, field producer and as a voiceover with particularly mellifluous tones. Finally he became obituaries editor.

He had an abiding enthusiasm for rock-climbing and mountaineering. He was closely involved in the coverage of Sir Chris Bonington's mountaineering expeditions, particularly in the Himalayas.

Hank moved to the Lake District in 1975 to concentrate on writing. He wrote several highly regarded books on climbing history and on other subjects as diverse as the American Civil War and the poet Samuel Taylor Coleridge, and made an acclaimed film on rock climbing *A Century on the Crags*.

He became something of a Keswick character. He was a keen tennis and squash player and his annual poetic contributions to the squash club dinners were legendary. As a lover of the theatre he worked for many years to ensure that live theatre continued in Keswick. He was an amiable eccentric, with a dry sense of humour, slow to criticize and quick with praise, an intellectual who wore his learning lightly.

Throughout his life he had a passion for books and literature, and this, combined with his love of the Lake District led to the series of articles, written for Cumbria Life magazine under the editorship of Keith Richardson, which appear in this book. In 1990 they were submitted for the BP Arts Journalism Awards and Alan was the runner up. This was a tremendous accolade for both writer and magazine. In being shortlisted for the awards, Cumbria Life overcame the challenging competition of many highly reputable national publications and, in the final analysis, out of 200 entries; Alan was second only to Fiona Maddocks, associate arts editor of The Independent newspaper.

There can be few areas in the country that have had such a rich and varied group of writers living and working within it and I hope that this book will serve as a tribute to them all, both past and present, and, of course, to Hank himself.

Joan Alexander
Keswick, 2008

CONTENTS

Beatrix Potter at the door of Hill Top.
Opposite: Hill Top seen from the garden.

Beatrix Potter and Hill Top

The tale of Beatrix Potter's life is more astonishing and moving than any of the stories she wrote. In the latter half of her life she was a happy, hard-working, North-country hill farmer, devoting herself to her husband and their home and to the breeding of Herdwick sheep. The first half of her life, however, from childhood to middle age, saw her the virtual prisoner of demanding and dominating parents. She was well looked after but denied all freedom and independence. She did not go to school. She could not go out and play. As a result, she had no childhood friends. In a sense, she had no childhood at all and it is a tribute to her powers of empathy that she was later able to write so tellingly for children. Most of the time she was alone in her upstairs room. When she was in company, it was exclusively adult, usually her parents. Their home life was quiet and rigidly controlled, following a regular daily routine in which punctuality was vital; serious and funless and claustrophobic. From the age of 14 until she was 30, Beatrix kept a diary, written in a code she had devised herself and in tiny hand-writing. The code was not cracked until the late 1950s, by Leslie Linder. The published *Journal* is a fascinating and revealing document. Beatrix was strong-minded and had a wide range of interests, but she held, or was held to her role as a dutiful and obedient daughter long after she had grown up. When she was nearly 40 and fell in love for the first time, with a perfectly respectable publisher, her parents refused to consent to her marriage.

It is hard to believe today but the repression of childhood was far from unusual in Victorian middle-class households. It took many forms. Often it was the result of religious bigotries; Samuel Butler and Edmund Gosse were among those who later wrote powerful accounts of that experience. The young Rudyard Kipling suffered exile from his family in India and the ferocious cruelty of an ill-chosen English foster-mother. Charles Dickens was tormented and humiliated as a child labourer in a London blacking factory. Countless little boys (like Hugh Walpole and Arthur Ransome) were despatched to boarding school to be beaten by the masters and mercilessly bullied by other boys. Elizabeth Barrett's life was so dominated by her father that she was forced in the end to deceive him by eloping with the poet Robert Browning. There are many examples and a surprisingly high proportion of them grew up to turn their experiences into high art, in autobiographies or thinly-disguised fiction.

Perhaps the closest parallel to Beatrix Potter's predicament was that of John Ruskin. He, too, had well-off parents and grew up in a house where all the work was done by servants and where everything ran with quiet, smooth, suffocating efficiency. He was not sent to school. He had no friends of his own age. He was indoctrinated in the puritan code: Obedience was a duty; life was earnest; he was allowed no toys and given no opportunities to explore the world for himself.

They were both exceptionally intelligent children, with lively minds and observant eyes and ears, and they reacted to the lonely and restricted lives imposed upon them in very similar ways. Driven in on themselves, they made the most of the enclosed worlds available. It gave them each an intense interest in tiny things, the beauty of their intricate patterns. Ruskin later said that he passed his days "contentedly tracing the squares and comparing the colours of my carpet, examining the knots in the wood of the floor, or counting the bricks in the opposite houses". Beatrix grew fascinated with shells and fossils, flowers and fungi, and made friends of such tiny creatures as she came across, moths, snails and mice. Their long hours of silence and seclusion taught them concentration. Each developed the ability to become totally absorbed for hours on end, reading or observing.

Quite early in life, they each showed remarkable talents as artists, reproducing what they saw in detailed and accurate drawings and watercolours.

There was another way in which both Ruskin and Beatrix Potter were fortunate in their strange upbringings. They were introduced to travel. Ruskin was taken on long annual journeys to France, Switzerland and Italy, where he saw things that were to dominate the rest of his life – the mountain scenery of the Alps, great French cathedrals, the architecture and paintings of Pisa and Venice. The Potters were not so adventurous but every year they took long summer holidays, at first in Scotland, later in the Lake District. On these holidays the young Beatrix enjoyed much greater freedom than she ever got at home in South Kensington – to roam the countryside, meet the farmers and villagers, and study the animals.

The Potters stayed at many houses in the Lake District, near Keswick, in and around Ambleside, by the shores of Windermere. One summer, when they had rented Wray Castle, they got to know the local vicar, Canon H.D. Rawnsley. He made friends with the shy girl and many years later, since he was the only person she knew who had had books published, she asked the canon's advice about a story she had written called *The Tale of Peter Rabbit*. He recognized its merits immediately, in the words and in the pictures she had drawn to illustrate them, and encouraged her to publish.

Beatrix was in her mid-30s. She went ahead and before long she was established as a highly successful writer of stories for young children. The money she earned gave her confidence, so much so that in 1906 she was sufficiently independent of her parents to buy herself a farm in the southern Lake District, Hill Top in the village of Near Sawrey. It was the first step in her magical transformation from submissive daughter to sturdy hill farmer.

The complete transformation took several years. At first she continued to live with her parents and hired a manager, John Cannon, to run the farm for her. But she spent as much time as she could in Sawrey, creating a flower garden, adding a small wing to the house, discussing the future development of the farm. In 1909 she bought an adjoining farm. Her adviser in these dealings was a local solicitor, William Heelis, and gradually they fell in love. Predictably, when she told her parents she was to marry, there was ferocious opposition. She was marrying beneath her, they said. But Beatrix had made her mind up and she and William were married in October 1913 to live together happily, ever after.

This marked the virtual end of her career as a serious writer. In the preceding twelve years she had written and illustrated nearly twenty story-books, all the tales which still give delight to the succeeding generations. As a writer, this was undoubtedly her golden period. The stories are told in a style that is simple, pure and elegant. She gives her animal characters human speech and activities, but they retain their true basic natures – cleanly or careless, reckless or calculating, timid or ruthless. Ginger the cat, serving in the grocer's asks someone else to serve the mice because it makes his mouth water too much: "I cannot bear to see them going out of the door carrying their little parcels". Beatrix Potter was a realist about life, animal and human. She had no sentimental illusions. Life is predatory, and it was this that gave the spice of menace (which children love, so long as they can also feel sure the ending will be happy) to her tales. The books had made her wealthy and famous, but now she turned resolutely away from all that to become a supportive wife and a serious farmer. She used the money to extend her empire, buying up fresh farms and thousands of acres of fell and herds of Herdwick. But she was not interested in the fame. When admirers came to gaze at her or ask questions about her writing, she dismissed them from her presence, often very brusquely.

In fact, in 1933, when Graham Greene wrote a perceptive essay about her work, taking it very seriously and giving high praise, she sent him an acid note, correcting some of the details and saying that she had no time for "the Freudian school of criticism".

She and her husband did not live at Hill Top but at a house

nearby. But she used Hill Top as her studio and study and it was here that she kept and displayed all the things she brought back from the shops and sales. They are still there, exactly as they were when she died in December 1943. She left everything, many farms and more than 4,000 acres, to her husband and stipulated that when he died it should all go to the National Trust. Her old friend Canon Rawnsley had founded the Trust and she was its most generous benefactor. She also laid down in her will that all "the rooms and furnishings used by me at Hill Top Farm" should be kept unchanged. Her wishes have been honoured. The National Trust opened Hill Top to the public in 1946 and it has been an increasingly popular calling place for the tourists ever since. Hill Top was built in the seventeenth century, a simple grey, working farmhouse with stone walls and a slate roof and flagged floors, approached from the village road by a stone path through a cottage garden. Beatrix Potter loved the place immediately. "It is a funny old house," she wrote in a letter, "it would amuse children very much. It really is delightful – if the rats could be stopped out ... I never saw such a place for hide and seek and funny cupboards and closets." The fight against the rats, who had taken the place over and had no wish to leave, was a long one, but she won in the end. Then she celebrated the house and described it and painted it in one of her stories, *The Roly-Poly Pudding (*later known as *The Tale of Samuel Whiskers),* which Graham Greene called 'her masterpiece.'

It is nearly half a century since Beatrix Potter died in 1943, at the age of 77. For thirty years Sawrey had been her home and hill farming had been her life. She was the first woman ever to be chairman of the Herdwick Sheep-breeders' Association. She cast away her earlier life of bourgeois respectability and repression. She was her own mistress now and, although rich and a great landowner, had no wish to keep up appearances. She spoke the dialect of the hill shepherds and wore sensible working clothes. One of her favourite stories was of how, one very wet morning, as she walked up a drove road to look at her lambs, she passed a tramp who called across to her: "It's sad weather for the like o' thee and me".

Enid Wilson

I got to know Enid Wilson, of Keswick, in the early 1970's. For more than twenty years she had been writing her short, clear, incomparable "country notes" column for The Guardian, two hundred words or so every fortnight, quiet in style but full of love and sympathy for Lake District life and lore, creatures and character.

I was not, at that time, particularly interested in that side of her life. I was putting together a book of photographs taken by the famous "Keswick Brothers", George and Ashley Abraham, pioneer rock climbers and professional photographers. George was Enid's father, and she gave me loads of invaluable information about him.

He had been a wonderful father, equable in temperament, cheerful and patient, a great lover of adventure and exploring, immensely knowledgeable about the countryside. Climbing to him, she said, was all about enjoyment. He did it solely for fun but he also did it carefully and sensibly, not showing off, refusing to be panicked, inspiring you with confidence. He was very strong in the legs and also very bow-legged. "Couldn't stop a pig in a blind alley," they used to say in the family.

Her Welsh mother was wonderful too, but in a very different way, a Bachelor of Science and an accomplished botanist, very artistic, with strong views on education.

As a result, Enid did not go to school until she was seven years old and then played truant as often as she thought she could get away with it. She was outdoors whenever possible, building up an intimacy and an empathy with the natural world – trees and plants, insects and birds and wild creatures of all kinds. She had her father's patience and her mother's knowledge, plus depths of observation and understanding that were special to herself.

Her father taught her rock-climbing on the little crags of Castle Head just outside Keswick. "Sometimes," she said, "he would put half a crown on top of a tricky boulder to encourage us to climb for it. It took me a long time to realize that no Abraham was going to put that sort of money on top of a rock if there was any danger of anyone getting it easily."

He was a pioneer motorist too. In 1900 or 1901 he was driving a Mabberley with tiller steering about the valleys, one of the first cars to explore Lakeland. Soon he was trying out new models for motoring magazines, and his two daughters were recruited into the testing team when they were still little girls. Enid was eight years old when she played an active part in what they claimed was the first motorized conquest of Wrynose and Hardknott passes. They were rough, unmetalled roads then and the whole family had to be ready to leap out of the Humber at the first word of command to stuff bits of old carpet under the struggling wheels.

Enid – the name was pronounced in the Welsh way with a light 'e' – was generous with the help she gave me, and I soon realized that her information was totally reliable, "What you get," she said in one letter, "will be authentic – no embroidery!" And that was entirely true and quite typical of her. She was a little, elderly lady but not at all frail, still full of energy and curiosity. Her manner was quiet, almost shy, but straight and clear and direct. When she talked about Lake District life, all aspects of it at all levels, it was with a calm authority. She knew what she was talking about – from a lifetime's close observation, and deep reflection, and much reading, and hours of leisurely

15

conversation with countless experts, farmers and huntsmen, fishermen and beekeepers and many more. She never lost the fascination she had felt from childhood for every detail of country life. It was this, and the sweet, simple freshness of her style that made her Guardian articles so addictive.

The story of how she got the Guardian job is very characteristic. She had never felt any great urge to get a job. She married soon after leaving school and was perfectly content to look after her husband, who worked in a Keswick bank, and bring up her two children and carry on studying the natural life of the Lake District. She knew the person who wrote the Keswick column for the Guardian, or Manchester Guardian as it then was, and when they died "my husband said, 'Why don't you do that?'" I said, "but I couldn't do that, I've never done anything seriously in my life." He said "try". So I wrote one or two and sent them off to A.J.Wadsworth who was The Guardian editor then and he said, Yes, I could try, and he put me on probation. I hope I'm still on probation, but I don't really know."

She had been writing the column continuously for nearly forty years when she told this story. It was very like her to see herself as still on probation after that length of loyal service. In the same way, at much the same time, she was very tentative when it was suggested that she should choose a selection of her pieces for publication as a hardback anthology, but fortunately she was finally persuaded and the delightful book Enid J. Wilson's Country Diary was published by Hodder and Stoughton in 1988, a few months before Enid died.

Though she was incorrigibly modest about her abilities as a writer, she took the work seriously. It was only two hundred words or so but she would ponder it for a long time, then scribble something down, then count the words and weigh the phrases, revise and prune and polish, until it was precisely what she wanted to say in a style as fresh and sparkling as the Borrowdale air on a spring morning. As the years passed she grew more and more accomplished. Great effort went into it but it read as easily and naturally as the leaves grow on the rowan. She developed the precious knack of honing a sharp, completely original phrase. She speaks of "this grudging spring," of the sheep "spreading in a grey fan up the lower slopes, on their way back to the high fells." She recalls "Old Tom," the Borrowdale policeman, "who would surge slowly into the pub at closing time on a Saturday night." She speaks of "the living twilight."

Enid was not anti-social, but she was not sociable in the conventional way. She liked to be out of doors in the hours of twilight or before dawn, on her own, hoping to see badgers or owls or to catch the "churring" song of the nightjars or the beginnings of the dawn chorus. No movement or sound or scent was too tiny for her notice. One of her nocturne pieces opened with the words: "I have always felt that people who live in the country and go to bed − or get up − at conventional hours miss more than they know."

Her favourite writer was Dorothy Wordsworth. She often referred to her in the column and quoted from the famous Grasmere Journal. They had many qualities in common, simplicity and unpretentiousness, fresh and vivid imagery, acute observation, complete respect for the individual identity and character of all natural objects and creatures. Each of them loved the world of nature for its own sake. In neither of them is there the slightest hint of the tweeness or sentimentality that you find in the Beatrix Potter stories, attributing human characteristics to rabbits and foxes and hedgehogs.

We find Dorothy's Journal fascinating partly, at least, for

the picture she gives of life at Dove Cottage with her beloved brother, the poet. Enid's brief was to portray the world around her, not herself, though her spirit often shines through, and when her anger was aroused – by the persecution of badgers, for example, or the greedy desecration of the landscape, or sloppy husbandry – there was no mistaking her feelings. Her canvas was a broader one than Dorothy's and her knowledge was more extensive and deeper.

Everything interested her. She had no illusions about the animal world, its constant hunger and sometimes savagery. Her undoubted favourites were the badgers, and she spent countless uncomfortable hours, lying silent and motionless on the fellside, being devoured by every passing insect, hoping for a brief sighting in the moonlight. But she loved otters too, and hares, owls and curlews, foxes and foxhounds, plants and trees, the whole of natural creation. Its naturalness was what she liked about it, everything simply getting on, without hang-ups or neuroses, with being what it was.

She liked people too – if they were natural. She often wrote about the Cumbrian folklore and customs, and passed many pleasant evenings in farm kitchens in quiet reflective "crack" with old friends. She relished the dialect: "How would you describe a woman who can never stop talking? Here she is a 'three-ha'penny rattle,' a 'bletherskite,' or even a 'chitterwallit', but does not really deserve criticism. Criticism is reserved for one who is a 'hard-feaced un,' 'a proper boiling bit' (remembering knuckle-ends of lamb) whose face 'wad spoil a pick'. How much happier to be labeled 'that nice, old fashint folk', or to be like the man who lives on the other side of Skiddaw. He is dumpy, shiny-apple cheeked, and smiling and is said to be a 'cheerful laal begger, he shines like a closet door on a frosty morning'."

Bishop Richard Watson

For the past two hundred years or so Bishop Richard Watson, who built Calgarth Park on the eastern shore of Windermere and lived there as a country gentleman in the days of Wordsworth and Coleridge, has had a lousy press. Time and again he has been reviled as a grasping and ruthless careerist, a Christian priest who did not believe in the divinity of Christ, who used contacts and influence to amass a large number of church jobs and the money from them while cheerfully ignoring all the duties they involved. He has also been abused as a Westmorland landowner who managed his acres entirely for profit, quite unconcerned about any environmental desecration that might result.

Above: Calgarth Park

Richard Watson

The chorus of condemnation was started by the journalist Thomas De Quincey, a neighbour of the bishop's in the early years of the last century and a frequent visitor to Calgarth Park where he was, by his own admission, always generously entertained. More than 20 years later, writing his brilliant but not entirely reliable Recollections of the Lake Poets, De Quincey repaid his former host with several pages of abuse. The bishop, he said, had been "a man remarkable indeed for robust faculties, but otherwise commonplace in his character, worldly-minded, and coarse even to obtuseness." He was egotistical and unprincipled, cynical about the Christian faith, interested only in material gain and status.

"All his public, all his professional duties he systematically neglected," he wrote.

He was also, De Quincey says, a bitter and discontented man, convinced that he had been cheated of the great glittering prizes (an archbishopric for example) that should have been his by merit.

The De Quincey line has been taken by nearly all those who have written about the bishop subsequently. George Atkinson, in his Worthies of Westmoreland, said that Watson had "lived and died without one act of charity or benevolence to show that he had lived." In this century H.A.L. Rice, in his Lake District Portraits, entitled his chapter about Watson "Absentee

Shepherd" and commented: "if the sheep committed to his care ever thought it worth their while to look up to him for feeding, they were fated for the most part to remain hungry." And so the bishop-bashing has continued, in countless books and articles.

It is not to be wondered at that the bishop's own memoirs should present a very different picture. The book is called Anecdotes of the Life of Richard Watson, Bishop of Llandaff. It was published in 1817, the year after his death. It deals, almost exclusively, with his public life – his appointments, publications, speeches in the House of Lords, letters on current issues – and says little about personal feelings or family life. It is very much what you might expect from the autobiography of an active and polemical public figure, an exercise in self-justification. The man who emerges from the account is exceptionally gifted, with an acute intelligence, hard-working and unashamedly ambitious, and also high-principled, anxious for promotion and recognition but never prepared to betray his principles to advance his prospects.

He makes an impressive case for himself. He was a clever and assiduous and articulate man. He was also, though he does not say this, very much a man of his times. In 18th Century England it was generally accepted, and expected, that an ambitious man would use his contacts and political "pull" to further his career and his fortune. This applied to clergymen as much as to other walks of life. William Howley, Bishop of London at that time and then Archbishop of Canterbury, was an accomplished 'pluralist,' collecting church jobs by the dozen, much more successful at it than Watson.

There are widely divergent views, then, about Bishop Richard Watson of Llandaff in South Wales and Calgarth Park, Windermere. Which view you take, whichever way you interpret the story of his life, it is a fascinating one. He was always proud of the fact that he came from an old Westmorland family of "statesmen," independent landowners in the Shap region.

His father, though, was not a farmer but a teacher, headmaster if Heversham School for nearly 40 years. Richard was born in 1737 and did well enough at his father's school to win a scholarship to Trinity College, Cambridge. He went as a "sizar," a poor scholar, that is, who had to work part-time as a college servant to pay his board and lodging. His fellow-students called him "the Westmorland Phenomenon" on account of his "blue worsted stockings and coarse mottled coat." But he worked hard and was a ready learner and before long he improved his situation by winning a college scholarship. He had a clear logical mind and a capacity for concentration. He was good at Latin and mathematics and natural philosophy, key subjects in those days. And he had a serious eye to the future. In his memoirs he wrote: "I had a strong ambition to be distinguished, and was sensible that, though wealth might plead some excuse for idleness, extravagance and folly in others, the want of wealth could plead none for me."

He took his degree and was proclaimed "second wrangler," the university's second best mathematician of the year. It was generally agreed that he would have been the outright winner but for blatant favouritism. There was something of a scandal and Watson was delighted. "The talk about it at the time did me more service than if I had been made senior wrangler," he wrote.

Trinity soon made him a Fellow and he got several college and university jobs, teaching and administering. He made dozens of contacts that were to prove invaluable in later life.

At the age of 27 he applied for the post of Professor of Chemistry, which to modern eyes seems an odd thing to have done since he knew no chemistry at all. But chemistry was a lowly discipline in those days and the post carried no salary, so there was little competition and he was appointed. In his memoirs he confessed cheerfully: "At the time this honour was conferred upon me, I knew nothing at all of chemistry, had never read a syllable on the subject; nor seen a single experiment in it; but I was tired with mathematics and natural philosophy...."

There was nothing shocking or even unusual about this in university life at that time, and the appointment was quickly vindicated. Watson plunged himself into this new field of study, hired an experienced assistant from Paris, and turned himself into an expert. Fourteen months later he was lecturing to packed lecture rooms. His various essays were turned into chemistry textbooks that sold well for many years. In 1768 he was made a Fellow of the Royal Society. He invented something called "the black bulb thermometer." The government asked for his advice on ways of improving gunpowder, and he suggested they should try making charcoal by distilling wood in enclosed containers. It worked, and the authorities reckoned it saved them £100,000 a year. Watson even contrived to persuade the government to grant £100 a year towards his professorship. If for nothing else, his name should be remembered gratefully as a pioneer founder of the Cambridge School of Chemistry.

In 1771 another great challenge presented itself. Cambridge's Professor of Divinity died. This was the most respected and the best-paid job in the university, and Watson had long coveted it. The fact that he knew little or no theology was not going to deter him. He frankly admitted that he "knew as much of divinity as could be reasonably be expected of a man whose course of studies had been directed to, and whose time had been fully occupied in other pursuits."

His many friends and admirers encouraged him to apply. The only trouble was that he had no degree in divinity and that was one of the qualifications. Amazingly, it took him just seven days – employing what he called "hard travelling and some adroitness" – to get himself fixed up with the required doctorate.

The very next day saw the examination of the candidates. Watson read a Latin dissertation on biblical themes and was elected unanimously. In his memoirs, written many years later, he congratulated himself.

"Thus did I, by hard and incessant labour for 17 years, attain, at the age of 34, the first office for honour in the university; and, exclusive of the Mastership of Trinity College, I have made it the first for profit. I found the Professorship not worth quite £330 a year, and it is now worth £1,000 at the least."

Money was always important to him, but there is no denying his remarkable intellectual abilities and his self-confidence.

As he had done with chemistry a few years before, he now made himself a master of divinity by rigorous study, concentrating on the Bible and the New Testament in particular. It may be true, as his critics have said, that he doubted Christ's divinity and did not believe in miracles, but much the same can be said of some 20th Century Anglican bishops, and Watson certainly made himself a powerful defender of Christ's message to the world, in sermons and speeches and printed tracts. His Apology for Christianity (1776) defended Christ and his church against the published views of the historian Edward Gibbon, and won praise from Gibbon himself who described Watson as "the most candid of my critics" and "a prelate of a large mind and liberal spirit."

Watson was a Whig, a supporter of the English constitution

as established by the 1688 revolution. He believed the powers of the monarch should always be held in check by the landed gentry. And he was not afraid to speak his mind. When the American colonists took to arms to free themselves from British rule, he preached a sermon supporting their case. Clearly this was going to upset King George 111 and might even have led to a charge of treason. Watson was not charged, however, and when the Americans won their war of independence and a Whig government came to power in London, he got his reward for his courage and outspokenness. Through the influence of the Duke of Rutland, he was appointed Bishop of Llandaff. It was a very ancient diocese but a very poor one too. But it gave Watson an impressive title and a seat in the House of Lords.

He enjoyed controversy, took a keen interest in current affairs, and could express himself lucidly and forcefully. On many of the great issues he took an enlightened line. He argued for union with Ireland; for the abolition of the slave trade; for a measure of parliamentary reform and also much-needed reforms in the ancient universities; he campaigned for the emancipation of Roman Catholics, who were still subjected to many restrictions. Even King George 111 according to contemporary accounts, held him in high regard. He once complimented Watson on some stand he was taking.

Watson said: "I love to come forward in a moment of danger."

The King replied: "I see you do, and it is a mark of a man of high spirit."

All this time he was improving his financial standing by picking up church jobs – as vicar or rector, prebend or archdeacon, all over the place – taking the money and paying some locum tenens about a quarter of the full rate to do the actual work. It sounds unscrupulous now but it was the way things were done in the easy-going 18th Century. He even delegated his duties as Professor of Divinity, but for this he had to pay two-thirds of his salary to the locum.

He married well too.

"My constitution was ill-fitted for celibacy," he wrote in his memoirs, "and as soon, therefore, as I had any means of maintaining a family I married."

His wife was Dorothy Wilson of Dallam Tower in Westmorland. They married in Lancaster in December 1773, and the next day he shot off to North Wales to pick up a sinecure rectory there.

He kept up his links with Westmorland and when a former pupil of his died in 1786 and left him a large estate, he sold it for well over £20,000, a vast sum at that time, and used the money to acquire 70 acres along the north-eastern shore of Windermere and then to build his country house at Calgarth Park. He said that ill health was forcing him to seek the country air, but there is no doubt that he also liked the idea of becoming a "statesman," a gentleman-farmer and a local worthy, extending and improving his estate. He threw himself into his new role with characteristic whole-heartedness. From this time to the end of his life he spent most of the year at Calgarth, and a few winter months in London.

In his memoirs he proudly claimed: "I made a large plantation, consisting of 322,500 larches on two high and barren mountains near the foot of Windermere. During the same period I improved above 150 acres of land, which was covered with heath, and not worth two shillings an acre. I know of no means more honourable, more certain, or more advantageous, of increasing a man's property, and promoting at the same time the public good, than by planting larches on mountainous districts and improving low waste lands by bringing them into tillage."

He had a large family – two sons and six daughters – and many friends, and was a genial and hospitable host. Among those who visited his mansion were William Wordsworth, Coleridge, De Quincey, John Wilson of Elleray and Walter Scott. Wordsworth, though, hated the larch tree as ugly, uniform and an alien intrusion, not a native of the Lake District. He hated them even more when they were planted by the thousand, in straight lines, up the sides of his beloved fells. He accused Watson of running a "vegetable manufactory."

The bishop was unrepentant.

"The cultivation of our mother earth," he wrote to a friend, "is the noblest way of providing for a family."

He put forward a scheme to drain Lake Windermere and use the land for agriculture, but this, mercifully, came to nothing.

De Quincey says that Bishop Watson only visited his Llandaff diocese three times in the 34 years of his reign. It is an exaggeration. He had to go there for a few days, once every three years or so, to preside over confirmations and ordinations. But he certainly kept his duties to the barest minimum and made no apparent efforts to do any pastoral work. Being bishop gave him the right to appoint cathedral officials, prebends. There were 12 such posts at Llandaff, each of them worth something in land or money, and eight of them were awarded to members of his family or Lakeland clergymen who were neighbours and friends of the bishop. This had the added advantage of enabling him to hold chapter meetings at Calgarth Park.

De Quincey also describes the bishop, in his later years, as discontented, a man who thought his abilities had deserved higher recognition. This is true, and Watson in his memoirs makes it clear that he felt he could have become Bishop of Durham and

Archbishop of York had he not been so principled. He condemns those clerics who crept and flattered their way to preferment, and says: "I was determined to be advanced in my profession by force of desert, or not at all."

He was unlucky in one respect: an outspoken Whig whose career developed at a time when the Tories were in power almost continuously.

He died in 1816 and lies buried in the churchyard at Bowness, where there is a memorial tablet to him by the sculptor Flaxman. His descendants continued to live at Calgarth Park for many years, adding two wings to the original house.

In World War 1 it was a convalescent home for Belgian wounded, then for British officers. After the war it became an orthopaedic hospital and school for crippled children, earning an international reputation. Since 1974, under a charitable trust, Calgarth Park has provided self-contained flats for elderly professional people.

The bishop is remembered there. A print of his portrait by George Romney stands in the entrance hall, and Olive Wilson, one of the residents, maintains a lively and informed interest in the controversial bishop and the house he built.

Hugh Walpole: Brackenburn

At the end of October 1923 Hugh Walpole was driving – or being driven rather, by his chauffeur – through the Lake District on his way to visit his family in Edinburgh. He was 39 years old, a bachelor, and already comfortably established as one of Britain's most prolific and popular novelists.

For all his success in the world, though, Walpole was a man who, in fundamental respects, had never really grown up. He was a prey to sudden, overwhelming enthusiasms, and also to sudden violent outbursts of temper. He could be impatient and

Above: Brackenburn with a view of Derwentwater beyond.

Hugh Walpole in the garden at Brackenburn

impetuous. He had not learnt, and was never to acquire, the cautious, considered manner that is generally taken to be the mark of an adult man of affairs. And so it came about, on November 1st, when he was taken to look at a house on the fell-side above the eastern shore of Derwentwater, he agreed to pay the asking-price without attempting to bargain or contemplate having it surveyed before he committed himself.

He wrote in his diary that night: *Day with a star indeed, because on it I bought what I hope will be the abode of my old age – Brackenburn, Manesty Park, Derwentwater. Came on it quite by chance – a stray remark from the owner of our Keswick hotel. Above Grange in Borrowdale. A little paradise on Cat Bells, running stream, garden, lawn, daffodils, squirrels, music room, garage, four bedrooms, bath – all! Nice people have it, the Richardsons. Entranced and excited.*

Walpole had loved the Lake District since the age of 14 when the first of many family summer holidays at a farm near Gosforth enabled him to forget for a while the terrors of life at boarding school. As a teenager he relished the fresher, colder air of the north and the freedom to explore by bicycle along the valley roads, on foot to the mountain tops. In his early adulthood he had met his need to escape sometimes from the cosmopolitan bustle, to write in uninterrupted quiet, by renting a cottage in Cornwall. Now, approaching 40, he wanted a more substantial place and one that he could mould to his own requirements. He found it in Brackenburn. Six months after his discovery of the house, working out his plans for its extension, he wrote: *I know this is where I am meant to come and work. It is like a divine call, if that's not being too egotistic, and I pray God I may do my very best here.*

Walpole paid £2,700 for Brackenburn – the house, its

detached garage with a music-room above, and more than one acre of steeply-sloping garden which was planted with trees and shrubs of various kinds and through which a stream tumbled. The price sounds ludicrously low to modern ears and it was certainly no problem to Walpole whose annual income ranged between £3,500 and £4,500. But what he got for his money was nothing like the estate as it stands today.

The house had been built in 1909 by the Richardsons, the family who now sold it. The job had been done with Edwardian thoroughness. The roof is Skiddaw slate and the thick walls are neatly constructed of slabs of stone from the Galt Quarry in Borrowdale, slanted slightly outwards so that rain water would not run inside. The back of the house butts hard into the hillside. On three sides, the house is effectively insulated by trees and shrubs. Only to the front, to the north–east, is it open to the weather and the wind blows only very rarely from that direction. Walpole was lucky. The survey he did not bother to have was not necessary. The house was solid. It was, as it still is, comparatively warm in winter, pleasantly cool in summer. But when Walpole bought it, it was scarcely more than a bungalow. Downstairs, there was a small hall, a sitting room, a dining room, two bedrooms, a kitchen and a bathroom. Upstairs was nothing more than one small bedroom.

He soon set about changing this. Walpole was a compulsive collector – books, paintings, sculptures – and a hospitable man. He needed room for his things and for his many guests. So he had the upper floor extended to provide two spacious bedrooms and a commodious bathroom: the sides of the bath were formed by handsome slabs of local slate. Downstairs, many bookshelves were built. In the sitting room, the three glass panels at the front of the bay window were replaced by one large picture window, framing the panoramic prospect across the lake to Keswick and its embowering mountains. Opposite this window, he had a large mirror hung (it is still in place) and tilted slightly forward to reflect the view from the picture window.

He had a central heating system installed and got a petrol engine to generate electric light. Mains electricity did not come to Borrowdale till more than 40 years later.

In the garden he harnessed the stream to feed two ornamental fountains and pass through a little slate-lined pool. He loved to lie in bed and listen to the running water. By the road below the house the Richardsons had built a garage, then a room above it which they called their music room. It is a handsome room, full of light, with windows on three sides and a view across the Manesty treetops to the lake and the crags and mountains beyond. Walpole covered the walls with bookshelves and made this his library and writing room.

From the first, his hopes that this would be the perfect place for him to work were blissfully fulfilled: *Across the lawn, looking over the wood – now fresh with spring green leaves – to the faint blue waters of the lake, I push back the door, go up the stairs to the room that levels the treetops, sit down, fuss with my paper and pen, look about me, and then, suddenly, my vision is filled once again, with that other world where I know every little street, the look of every hill, can hear the sound of sea crashing on the shore; figures move, first as shadows, then as it were seen from behind a window, then close to me – I hear their voices, know that they are living and true, and that I am one with them, and I begin once again to scribble on to paper what I see and hear: their vitality, their truth, these things are truly real to me while I write. Only when the last word has been written and a strange foreign thing between cloth covers appears on my table do I realize that I have once again been tricked, but already a new vision is opening up.*

It sounds idyllic and it was. Walpole was one of those very rare writers who actually enjoyed the process of writing. He was formidably fluent. He had a teeming and vigorous imagination, his gift for storytelling had been born out of great suffering – he was no longer bullied at school when his tormentors discovered that he could entertain them with wild and fascinating tales – but now it made him rich and famous and happy. He was, as he cheerfully admitted, a lucky man. The books and articles flowed easily from his open pen – in a way, all too easily for he had a naturally vague and imprecise mind and he was always too excited about the next project to spend time on revision. His style, as a result, is sloppy. But the characters are strong, larger than life: the action is dramatic, often melodramatic; he could evoke atmosphere, especially the sense of evil and cruelty and pain; his narratives had drive and pace.

Although he adored his new home, Walpole rarely spent more than three or four consecutive weeks there. The call of London life was too strong; he had to see his friends and catch up with the literary gossip; there were operas to attend in Europe; lectures and film scripts to be delivered in the United States. But when he needed to write, he returned to Brackenburn. And when he was not at his desk, he merged himself into local life. He explored the hills, admiring the ever-changing light, sometimes accompanied by the Keswick mountaineer and photographer George Abraham. He joined the Keswick Chess Club. He bought books from Mr. Chaplin. Gradually he resolved to express his gratitude to Cumberland and its folks by basing a major work on what he called 'this enchanted place.'

It was to be a new venture for him, a historical romance, a

family saga that would start in the early 18th century and stretch over four weighty volumes. "These books," he said, "shall clinch my reputation or I'll die in the attempt."

He was averaging one major novel a year and he liked to begin work on each new one on Christmas Eve. In 1927 he bought many books about 18th century English life, especially that in Cumberland, and soaked himself in the period. The shape of his first volume formed itself gradually in his mind. He meant it to be "a fine, queer book in the big manner." Finally on Christmas Eve, he took up his pen and wrote his opening words: *A little boy, David Scott Herries, lay in a huge canopied bed, half awake and half asleep...*

He had misgivings at first but before long the old reliable magic was at work. The story and his characters possessed his mind. In the spring of 1928 there was a long interruption but when he returned to Brackenburn and seated himself at his desk in the music room he found the fortunes of his dark hero, Rogue Herries, *came flooding back all day, and by evening had driven everything else of every sort from my mind.*

By the time *Rogue Herries* was published, to general acclaim, Walpole was equally immersed in its successor, *Judith Paris.* When he went to weekend with the Brett Youngs at Esthwaite, he was so intent on the story that they gave him a room to write in with a handsome view. He found this stimulated his imagination so freshly that he determined to create similar working conditions for himself at home. By this time the growing trees of Manesty had effectively cut him off from the Derwentwater prospect. So he had a further storey added to the garage building to make a spacious work room from which he could look across the tree tops to the moving surface of the lake. It was here in the next three years that *Judith Paris* was finished and the Herries Chronicle completed with the writing of *The Fortress* and then *Vanessa*. To obviate the distraction of long interruptions when the narrative was flowing, he had a lavatory installed behind the study. On the outside wall of the lavatory, a slate inscribed: 'H.W. April 17th 1930.'

Walpole had many best-sellers to his name but the Herries Chronicle surpassed them all, in popularity at least. All four volumes have been continuously in print now for more than half a century.

Throughout the 1930's Hugh Walpole enjoyed Brackenburn, maintained his prodigious productivity, and prospered. In 1934 he went to Hollywood to write the screenplay for M.G.M.'s 'David Copperfield.' In 1937 he was knighted in the Coronation Honours List. That same year he claimed a rarer distinction – he finally persuaded the National Trust to allow him, at his own expense, to have some of the trees of Manesty felled (they were once again obstructing his view) and replaced by shrubs.

After the destruction of his London flat by Nazi bombers, he spent more of his time in his Borrowdale home, working on two further instalments of the Herries story, *The Bright Pavilions and Katherine Christian* which he did not complete. In May 1941, although he was unwell, he insisted on marching through the rain at the opening of Keswick's War Weapons' Week and making a speech in Fitz Park. In the days that followed his condition deteriorated rapidly. He died in his bed at Brackenburn on the morning of June 1st.

For many years he had attended, when he could, the Sunday morning service at St.John's Church in Keswick, and he was buried there in a grave that looks westward towards Cat Bells and Brackenburn. He left his books about the Lake District to

Keswick Library; letters and manuscripts and pictures to the Fitz Park Museum. There was an hotel in the town named after him and a shopping precinct named after his most popular saga.

At Brackenburn everything is much the same as it was in his day. His fountains still work; the garden blooms; everything about his "little paradise on Cat Bells" has the air of being well looked after. What used to be called the garage is now separately owned and more grandly titled, Brackenburn Lodge. But the main house is hardly changed since Walpole's time. The structure appears as solid as ever, rooted in the rock; its situation is as impressive as it was on the day when it caught the heart of the impulsive novelist; and the view across the lake, which refreshed his fancy as he sat writing, remains unchanged.

Hartley Coleridge

Hartley Coleridge

Hartley Coleridge, the first child of the eminent poet and philosopher Samuel Taylor Coleridge, is rarely remembered nowadays. Very occasionally one of his sonnets or short lyric poems may appear in an anthology. A selection of his letters was published in 1936. The rest, as Shakespeare said, is silence. Tens of thousands of people go every year to the churchyard in Grasmere to gaze at the Wordsworth family graves and study the headstones, but I doubt whether there is one in every thousand of them who notices Hartley's grave just beyond – or if they do notice, would know the sad story that lies behind the simple statement: "Hartley Coleridge: 1796 – 1849."

It is not easy to be the child of eminent parents. The British royal tradition illustrates this admirably. Prince Charles, whose family troubles have made such a stir recently, is only the last (so far) in a long tradition of Princes of Wales whose lives have been overshadowed and blighted by the status they were born to and the pressures put upon them by their parents and position and the curiosity of the public. Winston Churchill once referred to himself as "the unhappy son of a distinguished father," though his problems sprang not from over-interference but from almost total parental neglect. As the world knows, Churchill triumphed over his inherited disadvantages, though his own son Randolph, notoriously did not.

For the young Hartley Coleridge things were not that bad. When he was born, his father was by no means a famous man though many of those who knew him already recognized that he was a remarkable man, as a writer and a speaker. The Coleridge marriage was young and still happy, and the little boy was much loved and cared-for. Coleridge pere had grown up in a big and cheery family in a country village near Exeter, but he was only nine when his father died and he found himself banished to a school in the city of London. He felt it as a rejection, and the scars of it, I think, damaged his personality irretrievably. The school was cold and brutal in its methods, the food was awful; he missed the warmth of family life and the freedom he had enjoyed to roam along the river-bank and through the woods and meadows near his home. When his own son arrived, he determined that he should have a very different childhood. He described this determination in a poem he wrote in the winter of 1797-8, *Frost at Midnight*.

The house has gone to sleep. All is quiet and Coleridge sits in the little front room of his cottage at Nether Stowey in Somerset, in front of the fire, with the baby Hartley asleep in the cradle at his feet. He recalls his own childhood trauma:

> …..*for I was reared*
> *In the great city, pent' mid cloisters dim,*
> *And saw nought lovely but the sky and stars.*
> *But thou, my babe, shalt wander like a breeze*
> *By lakes and sandy shores, beneath the crags*
> *Of ancient mountains, and beneath the clouds,*
> *Which image in their bulk both lakes and shores*
> *And mountain crags……*

Coleridge was never notable for keeping his promises, and he got worse as he got older, but this is one promise he did keep.

Two years after that poem was written, his closest friends, William and Dorothy Wordsworth, found a little cottage they could afford to rent in Grasmere and moved up there. Six months later – in order to be near them – Coleridge brought his wife and son to live in Greta Hall, the big new house above the River Greta in Keswick. So Hartley did grow up to run happily about in the country-side, with the river nearby and lakes and mountains and crags not far away, a child of nature.

He was, all the accounts agree, a brilliant and odd and delightful little boy. In his first ecstatic letters from Greta Hall, Coleridge repeatedly describes him as "a Spirit dancing on an aspen Leaf." A year or two later he wrote: "Hartley is what he always was a strange, strange boy, 'exquisitely wild,' an utter visionary, like the moon among thin clouds, he moves in a circle of light of his own making. Of all human beings I never saw one so utterly naked of self." He created an imaginary country which he called Ejuxria, and for which he devised a language and a constitution and laws. He was president of this land, and his inventive mind poured out complex stories. One visitor to Greta Hall, seeing Hartley in a thoughtful mood, asked him what the matter was. Hartley, aged eight, replied: "My people are too fond of war and I have just made an eloquent speech in the Senate, which has not made any impression on them, and to war they will go."

It is a most unusual syndrome. As a little boy Hartley could talk and think like a wise and mature man. But when he grew to adulthood and middle age, he went on cheerfully behaving like a child – wayward, impulsive, unpredictable, always at one remove or more from reality. He was a life-long dreamer. He inherited in full measure his father's irresponsibility and lack of resolution. It was not that, in the manner of Peter Pan, he deliberately refused to grow up. He simply did not change.

Wordsworth must have had some early inkling of this. Like everyone else, he was amazed at the precocious spirit of

Hartley as a boy. When Hartley was six years old, Wordsworth wrote a poem praising him as one "whose fancies from afar are brought," but going on to worry about the boy's future, what contact with the hard realities of adult life might do to such a sensitive soul:-

I think of thee with many fears
For what may be thy lot in future years.

It is another prophetic poem about Hartley. Events were to more than justify Wordsworth's anxieties about what would happen when, as he put it in another poem, "shades of the prison-house" of adulthood began "to close upon the growing boy."

In the very first years it must have been a considerable help and stimulus to the boy's mind to have a father like Coleridge. Hartley was introduced to a circle of brilliant young men who were more than happy to talk to him and answer his questions and listen to his visionary chatter. Coleridge began to teach him Greek. But when the boy was seven, the Coleridge marriage collapsed in acrimony and Coleridge abandoned the family home for Malta and London and a life elsewhere. He sent letters, and money when he could, and paid very occasional visits to Greta Hall, but from this moment on he was an absentee parent.

Mrs Coleridge was now left at Greta Hall with three young children, and the job of looking after them devolved upon the broad shoulders of her brother-in-law Robert Southey. In character and temperament, Southey was the almost exact opposite of Coleridge – a man of probity, patience, industry and self-control. For many years he sat daily behind his desk in Greta Hall, writing poems and histories and biographies and translations, magazine reviews and articles, to keep the money coming in to provide for the Coleridge family, his own ever-growing family, and several destitute aunts (maiden or widowed)

Hartley Coleridge at the age of 52

as well as a sizeable menagerie of dogs and cats. So Hartley grew
up in the midst of a lively extended family. He went to school at
Ambleside and did well enough to get a scholarship to Merton
College, Oxford.

At the university he impressed his contemporaries – dons
as well as fellow students – with his idiosyncratic manner, the
vivid flow of his conversation, the originality of his ideas and his
esoteric range of knowledge. His showing in the final
examinations was good enough to earn him a Fellowship at Oriel

College. His father, and many friends and well-wishers, were delighted to see him launched on a promising career.

It did not last long. The fellowship began with one year's probation and Hartley got drunk so frequently, neglected his college duties so blatantly, and talked so wildly in company, that at the end of the year, in the summer of 1820, he was asked to resign. He protested and pleaded. His father went to Oxford to add his weight to the pleas. But the authorities were adamant and Hartley had to go.

He lived awhile in London, working as a journalist, then returned to the central Lake District to establish himself as a "character" – tiny, dark-complexioned, quirky in manner, walking the lanes and footpaths at all hours and making sudden little darting runs, drinking in the pubs and entertaining the locals with his friendly wit and his facility at writing verses for special celebrations. It was now that the affectionate legend of 'Li'le Hartley' was formed. He became a persistent wanderer, often disappearing for days on end on what would now be called a "bender." No one worried over-much because, wherever he went, someone would undoubtedly take him in and look after him, until he wandered off elsewhere. He got occasional jobs, teaching or writing articles, and continued to write serious poetry. A volume of his poems was published in 1833, dedicated to his father. In the opening, dedicatory sonnet he recalled his father's promise in *Frost at Midnight*, that he would be brought up in touch with nature, and added these lines:-

> .....*the prayer was heard: I "wandered like a breeze,"*
> *By mountain brooks and solitary meres,*
> *And gather'd there the shapes and phantasies*
> *Which, mixt with passions of my sadder years,*
> *Compose this book. If good therin there be,*

That good, my sire, I dedicate to thee.

His father died the next year. Father and son were all-too-disastrously alike – intellectually original and brilliant, but temperamentally flawed, lacking in will-power and self-control, a prey to impulse. Opium was the father's incapacitating weakness; alcohol was the son's. William Wordsworth had to watch both men, both friends of his, destroy themselves. He did what he could for Hartley, frequently advising and admonishing him, always forgiving him and paying the debts he left behind at public houses. In a letter written in 1826 he described Hartley as "strangely irresolute... like most men of genius, little to be depended upon."

Hartley died in January 1849, Wordsworth just over a year later. Some 20 years after that Canon Rawnsley thought it would be a good idea to chat to people in the Grasmere/Rydal area who had known Wordsworth and get their recollections and impressions of the great man before they were lost for ever. He was shocked to find how many of them had not read a word of Wordsworth's and how many of them held Hartley in much higher respect: "I had considerable difficulty here, as in all my interviews with the good folk, of keeping to the object or subject in hand. For li'le Hartley's ghost was always coming to the front. 'Naay, naay I cannot say a deal to that, but ye kna li'le Hartley would do so-and-so. Li'le Hartley was t'yan for them. If it had been Hartley, noo, I could ha' tell't ye a deal.'" Some of them thought Hartley had written Wordsworth's poems for him. Others had no doubt that Hartley was by far the better poet. All of them recalled Hartley with affection, for his quaint ways, his love of music and parties and jokes and beer, for the sheer liveliness of his "crack."

Canon Hardwicke Drummond Rawnsley

In every field of British activity the Victorian period produced men of high confidence and incredible vitality. They operated at the top levels of excellence, often in several different areas of endeavour at once, always tirelessly. In these more effete times, it is enough to make one feel exhausted just to read about their lives and all the things they managed to do – men like John Ruskin (artist and critic, lecturer and social prophet), and Mr Gladstone (statesman, scholar, orator) and the novelist Charles

Above: Crosthwaite Vicarage

Dickens. There were dozens more like them, men who hurled themselves at life's challenges and never seemed to run out of steam. The outstanding example in Cumbria and the Lake District was Canon Hardwicke Drummond Rawnsley. One of his Keswick parishioners described him as "the most active volcano in Europe."

Grevel Lindop in his masterly Literary Guide to the Lake District sums up Rawnsley's accomplishments in these words: "......minor poet, disciple of Ruskin, patron of arts and handicrafts, conservationist, fighter for public access to the countryside, biographer, topographer and local historian, placer of monuments and inscriptions, indefatigable lecturer, joint founder of the National Trust, a generous, devout and socially-concerned clergyman who seems to have enjoyed every moment of his incredibly full life."

Rawnsley was a Lake District man by adoption, not by origin or upbringing. His family were old-established Lincolnshire folk, mostly clergymen, and he grew up at first on the banks of the Thames, then at Halton Holgate in Lincolnshire, where his father was rector and the Tennysons were near-neighbours and close friends. He went to Uppingham School where the head-master Edward Thring introduced him to the poetry of Wordsworth. The young Rawnsley immediately became a compulsive poet himself and spent several summer holidays exploring the vales and fells around Grasmere.

He went to Oxford, to distinguish himself more as an athlete than a scholar, though he took degrees first in Classics, then in Natural Science. The great Oxford influence on him, though, was that of the Slade Professor of Fine Art, John Ruskin, then at the height of his prodigious powers and fame as lecturer, teacher and inspirational figure. Rawnsley was one of the

Canon Rawnsley

undergraduates – Oscar Wilde, amazingly, was another – who risked the jeers and sneers of their contemporaries by going out to Hinksey to work on Ruskin's road improvement scheme there.

There was never much doubt that Rawnsley was going to be an Anglican cleric. It was the family tradition and it accorded naturally with his fervent, pious and beneficent spirit. He had a compelling urge to go out into the world and do good. He was sent to a very tough part of Bristol to try mission work, and found it hard. By his own account, he was "half parson, half policeman." But it was here, in 1877, that he published the first of nearly 40 books – A Book of Bristol Sonnets – and it was here, too, that he inaugurated his life-long career as a public campaigner. He fought to save an ancient church tower from destruction and, as so often in later years, he won.

He was ordained a priest in Carlisle Cathedral in 1877 at the age of 26, and sent to take up the living at Wray on the western side of Lake Windermere. He assumed his duties – preaching, pastoral, social – with the enthusiasm that he took to everything. He set up classes in wood-carving and launched a series of campaigns to stop greedy developers from destroying the special quality of Lake District life and landscape. There was a scheme to build a railway alongside Derwentwater and up to Borrowdale to the summit of Honister Pass to transport slate from the quarry there to Keswick. There was a scheme to push a railway into Ennerdale. There were plans to extend the line from Windermere to Ambleside. Rawnsley organized the protesting pressure-groups, did the bulk of the work himself, and prevailed in every case. He created The Lake District Defence Society. He was a formidable force and made, not surprisingly, many enemies. One man, who had worked for him as a gardener, said he was "a peppery old devil." But he was effective and in those days, long before the formation of The Friends of the Lake District, there was an urgent need for such a tenacious and skilful defender of the District.

It was during those first pastoral days at Wray that he met and made friends with some rich visitors from London. Mr Rupert Potter and his family, who had rented Wray Castle for their summer holidays. He made particular friends with the dutiful daughter, Beatrix. He shared her interest in botany and was the first published author she had ever met. Nearly 20 years later she showed him a story she had written to amuse some children she knew, and he was impressed by her words and her illustrations, and encouraged her to publish. The little book was The Tale of Peter Rabbit, an immediate success and the first of many such stories that have an evergreen appeal to children. It was the money she earned by these publications that enabled Miss Potter to transform her life and become, very happily, a Lakeland sheep farmer. She did not forget her debt to Canon Rawnsley.

In the summer of 1883 he transferred to the living of Crosthwaite, Keswick's parish church, and he and his wife Edith moved into the old vicarage, their home and the centre of their work for the next 34 years. The house still stands on a superb hill-top site that commands fine southward views to Derwentwater and the Newlands fells. The poet Thomas Gray had stayed there in October 1769, on his seminal trip to the Lake District, and had written to a friend: "I got to the Parsonage a little before sunset, and saw in my glass a picture, that if I could transmit it to you, and fix it in all the softness of its living colours, would fairly sell for a thousand pounds. This is the sweetest scene I can yet discover in point of pastoral beauty; the rest are in a sublimer style." Rawnsley had these words incised into a slab of stone which he set in the terrace wall of the top of the handsome, sloping garden.

His first step was to establish a parish magazine, in the first issue of which he gave this promise to his new flock: "I shall come to Crosthwaite not only as an ecclesiastic and Church official, not only as a minister and superintendent of the religious services in church, mission room and Sunday school….. I shall come as one who holds himself pledged to encourage all good work, and who will try – God helping him – to preach that best of sermons among his friends and fellows – the life of Christian justice, temperance, tolerance and charity."

It is a true statement of his creed. He lived at a time when many Anglican priests tortured themselves continuously with doctrinal doubts and difficulties, submitting themselves and those around them to hours of angst about whether they stood in exactly the right part of the wide Christian spectrum. Rawnsley had no such troubles. His faith was simple, direct and practical, based on the words of Jesus. If he ever suffered doubts, he did not display them. He looked after his own family, cared for his parishioners, and in local and national affairs of many kinds he fought the good fight with courage and cheerful persistence and great industry.

When local landowners, on Latrigg and at Fawe Park, blocked off an ancient public right-of-way, he organized mass demonstrations and forced the removal of the barriers. He campaigned hard against the idea of a railway to the summit of Snowdon, one of the few fights that he lost. In 1900 he ran the campaign of protest against a plan to establish an electric tramway between Bowness and Ambleside, and this one he won.

Perhaps the most important of his achievements, certainly the one for which he is chiefly remembered today, was the formation of the National Trust. It was in 1893, when the land around Lodore Falls and the island of Grasmere were both up for sale, that he launched the notion that such places should be public property and carefully conserved. He talked it over with an old friend, the philanthropist Octavia Hill and a legal expert, Sir Robert Hunter, and soon The National Trust for Places of Historic Interest and Natural Beauty was established, with Rawnsley as its secretary. He remained its secretary – and its dynamo – until the end of his life.

It was he, in 1902, who raised £6,500 in five months to purchase Brandlehow Woods below Cat Bells, the Trust's first property in the Lake District, to allow public access to the shores of Derwentwater. Four years later he raised £12,800 to acquire 750 acres of Gowbarrow Fell above Ullswater. The ball was well and truly rolling, and has gone on rolling ever since so that nearly a century after its foundation, the National Trust owns and safeguards more than a quarter of the Lake District. Always happy to transpose his thoughts into a few lines of verse,

51

sometimes serious, sometimes light he wrote:

"I came and preached until I bust
The sacred name of the National Trust."

All the time he was writing – letters and sermons, lectures and articles, occasional poems and countless sonnets. To the modern reader, the sonnets are the great stumbling block. There are thousands of them, all of them serious and high minded, each of them carefully crafted, every single one of them, as far as my researches go – dull and lifeless. He was attempting the Wordsworth note and he simply could not do it. His prose writings, too, are frequently uninspired – long descriptive pieces about Lakeland vistas and sunsets, couched in a self-conscious "poetical" language and often spilling over into the mushy sentimentalism that the Victorian readers could take. But he had a clear, flowing, undemanding style, and when he was dealing with Cumbrian history, and local folk lore, and the literary associations of the Lake District, he could be informative and entertaining. His masterpiece, in my view, is an article he wrote to be read to the annual meeting of the Wordsworth Society in 1882 which he entitled Reminiscences of Wordsworth among the Peasantry of Westmoreland.

He had the bright idea, when he was still a young vicar at Wray, of seeking out the old folk of the Grasmere/Rydal area who had memories of Wordsworth and getting them to tell their tales. It is a funny, fascinating and revealing report, invaluable in the sense that had Rawnsley not done the research when he did, the information he gathered would have been lost for ever. He had a sharp ear and quickly mastered the art of reproducing the local dialect sounds, in speech and on the page. He also had the art of getting people to speak frankly, and their recollections and assessments of "Wudsworth", as they called him, are vivid and often surprising. None of them read his poetry or rated it at all. Most of them much preferred that of Hartley Coleridge, and some believed that Hartley really wrote the poems for which Wordsworth had been given all the credit. Others thought Dorothy Wordsworth had written the poems. But many recalled the old poet walking the alley lanes, speaking to no one, but mumbling noisily to himself as he went along, trying out the lines he was working on and frightening the local children. He was stiff and stand-offish – "not a man as could crack wi' fwoaks" – and one old man, who had delivered butter to Rydal Mount as a lad, delivered this terrible judgment: "a desolate-minded man, ye kna… It was poetry as did it…. His hobby ye mun knaa, was potry. It was a queer thing, but it would like eneuf cause him to be desolate…."

Soon after they moved to Keswick it occurred to Rawnsley and his wife that there was a need for some sort of useful occupation that would help to keep the working men and boys of the town out of the pubs on the long winter evenings. Rawnsley was a dedicated teetotaler, always on the look-out for positive ways of distracting his weaker brethren from the temptations of the demon drink. So they started evening classes, three nights a week in the parish rooms, giving instruction in painting and wood carving and metal work. It was part of the Ruskin message, the need to keep alive the traditional craftsmen's skills, to preserve the dignity of labour in the teeth of the ever-encroaching factory system of machines and machine-minders. It was a great success. After four years, their classes had nearly 70 regular attendants. So they decided they needed their own building, raised the money, and in 1894, opened the Keswick School of Industrial Arts. It flourished until a few years ago, when it was transformed into La Primavera, an Italian restaurant.

For seven years Rawnsley served on Cumberland County Council, campaigning vigorously for footpath preservation, proper signposts and public health measures. He was particularly concerned over tuberculosis which was a great scourge in those days, fighting for strict controls over the purity of the milk supplies and organizing the setting up of the sanatorium above Threlkeld. Later in life he was a ferocious campaigner against the new fashion for white-bleached bread, which he denounced so roundly that he was threatened with an action for libel.

Animal welfare was another of his causes. He fought against vivisection, rabbit-coursing, and the mass slaughter of birds for their plumage.

He fought, too, against the rising flood of dirty novels, magazines, photographs and vulgar seaside post-cards which, he proclaimed, were "poisoning the nation's character at its fountain-head", in other words by corrupting its young. It often seems as if Rawnsley's influence was negative – preventing developments in the Lake District, urging the suppression of pornography. He certainly wanted these measures taken, but he knew the importance of being positive as well. So he pressed for properly-run, free public libraries and worked hard to improve education, especially at Keswick School. In 1907 he formed the Secondary Schools Association, and acted as its secretary until his death. And he was an enthusiastic celebrator. It was he, in 1885, who launched the May Queen procession and festivities in Keswick, which the town still celebrates. And he loved bonfires. On June 22, 1887 he presided over the bonfire on the summit of Skiddaw to mark the Queen's Golden Jubilee. Ten years later, for her Diamond Jubilee, he organized 2,584 bonfires across Great Britain. It is said that from the summit of Skiddaw he was able to see 148 of his other bonfires cheerfully blazing.

He was a compulsive commemorator too; always ready to arrange for an inscribed stone to mark some significant piece of local history. In 1881 he saw to the setting-up of the Brothers' Parting Stone, marking the point where William Wordsworth said goodbye to his sailor brother John at the top of Grisedale Pass. When Ruskin died in 1900, Rawnsley organized the monument on Friar's Crag. There were many more, and it is entirely appropriate that Rawnsley should have his own tributary stone alongside the path between Friar's Crag and the Keswick boat-landings.

It is not surprising that, in the midst of all this activity, he should suffer occasional breakdowns in health, brought about by over-work. His solution was to take long trips abroad – to the Holy Land, the Alps, Greece and Italy, the United States – and when he returned home, fully recovered, he would give lectures about his experiences.

In 1893 he was appointed an honorary canon of Carlisle Cathedral. A few years later he was offered the bishopric of Madagascar but, after long thought, he gave way to the importuning of many friends and opted to stay in Keswick.

His wife Edith died in 1916 and Rawnsley retired a few months later, to live at Allan Bank – the Wordsworths' old home in Grasmere. He re-married in 1918 and continued to keep himself busy – designing war memorials, organizing bonfires to celebrate peace – until his death in May 1920.

He left Allan Bank, of course, to the National Trust.

Just over 20 years later the Trust received another and much greater bequest. In her will Beatrix Potter, remembering her old debt to Canon Rawnsley, left them more than 4,000 acres of fell farmland and many hundreds of Herdwick sheep.

It is hard to think of anyone, at any time, who had a more

powerful influence over Lake District affairs of all kinds than Hardwicke Drummond Rawnsley, an influence that was almost entirely beneficial. There ought to be a full-length, fully-documented biography of him. But there is not, nothing more than a brief, uncritical account of his life by his second wife Eleanor that was published in 1923. Several writers have proposed a biography, but no publisher has warmed to the idea. Well, publishers are like that. But Canon Rawnsley was a persistent man, and his memory is persistent too, and his time will surely come . . . .

Eliza Lynn Linton

Eliza Lynn Linton was born in 1822 at the Old Vicarage, Keswick. Her father, James Lynn, was vicar of Crosthwaite. When she died in 1898, her ashes were scattered alongside her father's grave in Crosthwaite churchyard. She was well-known in her day, the hey-day of Victorian England, as a popular novelist and a tough campaigning journalist, the friend and acquaintance of many leading literary figures, including Walter Savage Landor, Charles Dickens, W.M. Thackeray, Henry James and Rider Haggard. She wrote an excellent guidebook to the Lake District, and left a vivid – if not particularly complimentary – portrait of the Keswick region in the early part of the 19th

Above: The view from Crosthwaite Vicarage.

century. Yet, virtually no one reads her today, and there are very few who remember her name at all.

She had a terrible start in life. The youngest of 12 children, her mother died when she was a few months old and her father made no secret of the fact that he abandoned all responsibility. When the Bishop of Carlisle asked him what he meant to do for the children, he replied: "Sit in my study, my lord, smoke my pipe, and commit them to the care of Providence." So Eliza was bullied by the other children, received no education, and only came into contact with her father when he was beating her for some misdemeanour.

It is the sort of family background that modern sociology regularly advances as an explanation and excuse for extreme forms of adolescent and adult depravity. Amazingly, it seems to have done Eliza no harm. She could soon read and she read voraciously and taught herself several foreign languages. She was intelligent and observant and developed an independent spirit.

The family moved from Keswick to Kent – a house called Gad's Hill on the London-Dover road - when she was nine years old, but she never forgot the landscape of her childhood. Once grown up, she defied her father's wishes and launched into a career as a novelist. She was not very successful at first but, sustained by an annual allowance from her father, she persisted and before she was 30 had a full-time job as a journalist on the *Morning Chronicle.* Women had written for newspapers and magazines before but she was the first to get a staff job in journalism. At first she was paid 20 guineas a month. Soon she was earning more, writing articles and reviews for various magazines, including Charles Dickens' *All the Year Round.*

It was about this time that she came to know Thackeray,

another novelist and magazine editor, and formed a perceptive view of the two contrasting characters: "Thackeray, who saw the faults and frailties of human nature so clearly, was the gentlest-hearted, most generous, most loving of men. Dickens, whose whole mind went to almost morbid tenderness and sympathy, was infinitely less plastic, less self-giving, less personally sympathetic. Energetic to restlessness, he was a keen man of business and a hard bargainer, and his will was as resolute as his pride was indomitable."

Eliza Lynn Linton

She was a clear-eyed observer and a forthright writer and there were times when Dickens felt that her articles were altogether too outspoken, especially on sexual questions, for his middle-class readership. Eliza was a tireless campaigner for female emancipation, a pioneer in that field, but she had no time for the strident extremists of the feminist cause who, she thought did more harm than good. In an article called *The Girl of the Period,* written in 1868, she attacked the idea of the modern woman: "... a creature who dyes her hair and paints her face... a creature whose sole idea of life is fun; whose sole aim is unbounded luxury... She lives to please herself, and does not care if she displeases everyone else."

In 1858 Eliza married W.J.Linton, a wood-engraver and minor poet. Two years before she had sold the old family home, Gad's Hill, to Dickens for £1,790. Her home now was in London, but her husband had a big dilapidated house on the shores of Coniston Water, called Brantwood, and they spent much of their time there, together with his seven children from a previous marriage.

It was an anarchic, feckless household, not greatly to her fastidious taste, but she and her husband collaborated to produce a guide book called *The Lake Country*. He did the illustrations and she wrote the words, and, although much of her information is naturally mistaken or misleading to the present-day reader, it is still full of fascination and her fluent, ironic style makes it a pleasure to read. This is how she introduces it: "It is long since any book was written descriptive of the Lake Country. Green, and West, and Mrs. Radcliffe, and others of the Picturesque School, gave their absurdly exaggerated accounts of what they saw and periled in those 'inhospitable regions,' as it was then the fashion to call them; but when the reaction against romanticism set in, and people learnt for themselves that the ascent of Blencathra could be made without a fit of apoplexy and the necessity of blood-letting midway – that Borrowdale had nothing maniacal in it, and that Newlands was rather lonesome but not in the least degree terrifying – then all this idealistic writing was at a discount, and only guide-books containing useful road-side information were asked for ... It seemed to my husband and myself that a pleasant book could be made by treating the Lake

Country with the love and knowledge – artistic and local – belonging of right to natives and old inhabitants."

And that is what they did.

The picture she gives of the Lake District – its varied landscape, its history, the flora and fauna and points of special interest – is a flattering one. Which is more than can be said for the picture she paints of Keswick (in the 1820s and '30s) in another of her books. This is a three-volume novel which she called *The Autobiography of Christopher Kirkland,* published in 1885. The central figure is male and the format is fictional, but there is no doubt that it is a thinly-disguised account of her own life. And Keswick emerges as a most disgraceful place: "...there were 17 public houses and jerry-shops; and the man who did not get drunk would have been the black swan which the white ones would soon have picked to death. No one, however, tried the experiment of sobriety. There was no sense of public decency, no idea of civic order and as little of private morality. The parish-constable would have thought twice before taking up a crony for any offence short of murder; and then he would have left the door of the lock-up ajar. Not a man would have held himself justified in marrying before the woman had proved her capacity for becoming a mother..."

Things got worse when there was an occasion for celebration: "There were for the most part 'murry-neets' – dances in barns and public houses, where the men got drunk, the women fuddled and the marriage ceremony was discounted all round – and the Saturday-night fights, which came as regularly as the Sunday-morning shave."

The town, according to Eliza's description, was full of burglars and poachers, smugglers and even grave-robbers. There were village idiots "who could do nothing but sit in the sun and make mouths at those who passed." Even in church, the Keswickians could not be relied upon to behave properly: "... the pews were the familiar old cattle-pens of every size and shape, wherein the congregation sat in all directions and went to sleep in the corners comfortably ... at the feet of the choir, in the dark at the west end, the High School boys and girls sat on benches which every now and then they tipped up or overturned, played marbles, had free fights, laughed aloud and were dragged out by the hair, kicking and yelling, when their conduct was too obstreperous for even the lax reverence of the rest to bear."

There is probably more than a touch of novelist's licence in this, some exaggeration to give a livelier effect. Four or five years after writing that novel she decided to journey north and look again at her childhood home. By this time the redoubtable Canon Rawnsley lived at the Old Vicarage and he was delighted to let her look round the house and the garden. Some time after the visit she wrote to John Fisher Crosthwaite, a prominent Keswick figure: "Oh, how I wish I was young and strong for just a year, and could go down to Keswick, climb all the mountains, go over all the passes, skate on the frozen lake (I would not despise Blea Tarn, where we used to go and slide), go along the Skiddaw Terrace Road, and row about the lake as we used to. Whenever I am not quite well I dream of the lanes and roads about that fairest temple of nature (to me), chiefly of walking in the Limepots or else on the road just opposite the vicarage, I remember it all so vividly as it was ...."

Her marriage had broken up. They were incompatible characters: She was straight, sensible and meticulous while her husband was reckless, a political fanatic with very radical attitudes, and hopelessly, irresponsible in his domestic life. So they parted, without recrimination, and went their separate ways, he to a new life in the United States of America. They sold the house by Coniston to John Ruskin, Slade Professor of the Fine Arts at Oxford, and it was he who created the handsome house we see there today.

Eliza went on working hard, writing more and more novels that proved increasingly popular, countless articles for the *Saturday Review* which maintained her controversial reputation, and letters to her many friends. Among those friends was the great Bacon scholar, John Spedding of Mirehouse, Bassenthwaite Lake.

To the end she continued to battle for a fair deal for women, and maintained her feud against the feminist campaigners – "the shrieking sisterhood," she called them – who seemed to her to want women to solve their problems by becoming men.

She refused to use the new-fangled typewriters. In her final years, past the age of 70, she was still spending four or five hours each day at her desk, her pen moving steadily across the page. She died in London in July 1898.

Fox How: Dr. Thomas Arnold

At Christmas 1831, Dr Thomas Arnold, already beginning to build his reputation as the reforming headmaster of Rugby School, took his wife, Mary, and their seven young children for a holiday at Rydal in Westmorland. He wrote excitedly to a friend: "We are actually here. The higher mountains that bound our view are all snow-capped, but it is all snug and warm and green in the valley – nowhere on earth have I ever seen a spot of more perfect and enjoyable beauty, with not a single object out of tune with it, look which way I will ... close above us are the

Above: Fox How

Wordsworths."

For several years, Dr Arnold had been an admirer of Wordsworth's poetry. He had made the poet's acquaintance on earlier visits to the Lake District. Now the two men walked together almost every day, locked in earnest conversation, and spent many evenings exchanging visits. Although Wordsworth was a generation older and much more reactionary in his views, they enjoyed each other's company and were soon close friends. After this, the Arnold family came to the Grasmere/Rydal region every holiday, and in 1833 the doctor decided to build himself a second home there. Wordsworth held strong views about the sort of building that was appropriate to the Lake District, and threw himself whole-heartedly into the project. It was he who found the site, on the western side of the River Rothay, just north of Ambleside. The place was called Fox How. Dr Arnold bought 20 acres of rising ground, and his friend was generous and voluble with his advice about the house and the landscaping of the garden.

Half a century later, when Canon Rawnsley was asking local folk for their memories of Wordsworth, he came across a waller called George who had worked on the building of Fox How. George remembered Wordsworth's role vividly. "Well, he and the doctor was much I' yan anudder's company," he recalled. "And Wudsworth was a girt un for chimleys, had summat to say in the makkin' of a deal of em hereabout. There was 'maist all the chimleys Rydal way built efter his mind. I can mind he and the doctor had girt argiments aboot the chimleys time we was building Fox How, and Wudsworth sed he liked a bit o' colour in 'em. And that the chimley coigns sud be natural headed and natural bedded, a lile bit red and a lile bit yallar. For there is a bit of colour I' t', quarry stream up Easedale way. And heed a girt

Dr. Thomas Arnold

fancy an' aw for chimleys square up hauf way, and round t'other. And so we built 'em that road."

Many of the chimneys in the region are built to the poet's prescription, including those of Fox How. The building work was completed by the spring of 1834 – a big, spacious, two-story, four-square house, solidly constructed in Westmorland green-stone. Downstairs there was a large, handsome drawing room which gave a fine view across the valley to Fairfield. There was also a dining room, a school room for the children, and a study for the doctor. There were six bedrooms upstairs for the family and visiting friends, as well as two staff bedrooms and attics. Five acres of the land around the house were landscaped into a garden with lawns, flower beds, a lily-pond, many fine trees and shrubs. The rest of the land was left wild. It was a wonderful place for adventurous children.

Both house and garden are, in appearance, much the same as they must have been a century and a half ago. It is still privately owned. High up on the south front you can read the original datestone: *T and M Arnold, 1833.*

Below it there is now a burglar alarm, and on the roof – among the Wordsworth approved chimney stacks – you can see the only other sign of the 20th century, a television aerial.

Dr. Arnold was a man of restless conscience, immensely earnest and intensely busy. At Rugby he was engaged full-time in reforming and transforming the English public school system. It was badly needed. The public schools had fallen into corrupt and vicious ways, relying on the whip for classroom discipline and, for the rest of the time, more or less abandoning the boys to their own jungle laws. Thomas Arnold was a priest and a devout Christian. Education, to his mind, had two purposes, godliness and good learning, and the greater of these was godliness. It was important that the boys should master the grammar and syntax of the dead classical languages, Latin and Greek, and know something of their literatures. But the vital thing was that they should be inoculated with the Christian ideals, that they should grow up to be men of honour, integrity and truth. To this end, the headmaster surrounded himself with teachers who were good scholars and also men of strong moral character. He enlisted the active help of the senior boys who received special privileges when they reached the sixth form, but who were then expected to set a high-principled example to their juniors. Every Sunday afternoon the whole school assembled in the chapel and heard a 20-minute sermon from the headmaster. Few of them ever forgot the impact of that occasion. Thomas Hughes, in his famous novel *Tom Brown's Schooldays* which is closely based on his own schooldays at Rugby, described the doctor's pulpit style. "It was not the cold clear voice of one giving advice and warning from serene heights, to those who were struggling and sinning below," he said, "but the warm living voice of one who was fighting for us and by our sides, and calling on us to help him and ourselves and one another."

In addition to this, Dr Arnold was engaged in continuous theological debate, arranging the publication of his sermons, writing a book about Thucydides and the Greek language and researching for a book about the history of Rome. He was also attending to his expanding family. And keeping his many friendships in good shape by assiduous letter-writing. For a man so involved and restless, a holiday home in the Lake District fells was a necessary haven. For the family, it soon became a recurring delight.

By 1835 the family was complete, with nine lively children. The eldest of his five sons was Matthew, destined to become a fine poet and an outstanding critic, both literary and social. To modern ears, the holiday regime at Fox How may sound repressive. There were rules of behaviour which had to be observed by all. Each day had a rigorous routine, and punctuality was required. Father woke them all up at seven in the morning. They washed and went down to breakfast and family prayers. At 10 am there were lessons – Latin, Greek and History. Before lunch, everyone had to help with the housework, but after lunch, if the weather was good, they were free to go out and do whatever they liked – fell walking, boating on the lake or swimming in it, sliding or skating when the surface froze, even snipe-shooting, sometimes helping with the gardening. Then it was tea-time and after that the family gathered to hear father reading poetry, or play games, or to act out little plays. Bed-time varied according to age but they were all happily exhausted by the time it came.

Dr Arnold loved it there, all the more because he found the countryside around Rugby dull. He looked forward to his retirement, when he might live the year round in Rydal. In 1840 he wrote to a friend: "I sometimes think that if I were at all in nervous spirits, the solemn beauty of this valley would be almost overwhelming, and that brick streets and common hedgerows would be better for me; just as now, whilst my life is necessarily so stirring and my health so good, there is an extreme delight in the peacefulness of our life here, and in the quiet of all around us." Moral reservations would keep on breaking through. It is characteristic that he found Fox How "a home so peaceful and delightful that it would not be right to make it one's constant portion."

Dr. Arnold often preached at Rydal church and the friendship with the Wordsworth family was maintained, though the two men continued to take opposing views, on their frequent walks together, about education, politics and religion. "I love Arnold," Wordsworth told a friend. "He is a good man, an admirable schoolmaster, but he would make a desperate bad bishop." In the late 1830's the doctor and his two eldest sons, Matthew and Thomas, went to a public meeting at the Lowood Inn called to protest against the proposed extension of the railway from Kendal to Windermere. Wordsworth was there, too, and spoke at length. The boys thought the old man, long-winded, rambling and over-sentimental.

The doctor's hopes of being able to retire to Fox How were not fulfilled. He died at Rugby in June 1842, one day before his 47th birthday. He felt, of course, that there was much more still to be done. But the great work had been accomplished already, and his soul went marching on for generations. The school he created became the pattern for English upper-class education for the rest of the century.

Fox How went marching on, as well. Mrs. Arnold, a remarkable woman in her own right, moved there and for many years it was the centre of her ever-expanding family. The children grew up and married, and the name of Arnold became linked with other formative names of the Victorian age, the Arnold-Forsters, the Trevelyans, the Huxleys.

In April 1850 the two youngest Arnold girls, Susanna and Frances, were walking along the valley when they looked up the hill to Rydal Mount and saw the curtains being drawn. They knew then that their father's old friend had died. In December that year, a new friend, Miss Harriet Martineau, of The Knoll in Ambleside, came to dine at Fox How and brought with her a shy and awkward little woman whose name was Charlotte Bronte. Matthew Arnold, already pursuing a successful career, was home for the holidays, and Miss Bronte did not approve of his "seeming foppery."

A few years later a grandchild, Mary, was growing up at Fox How, meeting the eminent visitors and running wild – as the young Wordsworth had done – about the fells. When she grew up, she became the best-selling novelist of the last decades of the century, under her married name, Mrs. Humphrey Ward. In one of her books she described Westmorland as a "land at once of mountain solitude, and of a long-settled, long humanized life."

Dr Arnold's youngest daughter, Frances, later known to everyone as 'Aunt Fan,' continued to run Fox How as a welcoming haven for the widespread family until her death in 1923 at the age of 90.

Greta Hall

There can be few houses anywhere in the world that are so rich in distinguished literary associations as Greta Hall in Keswick; hardly any that have been so variously and tumultuously 'lived' in by eminent men. From 1800 to 1803 it was the home of Samuel Taylor Coleridge, poet and philosopher, friend and inspiration to Wordsworth. He left Greta Hall in December 1803 and for the next 40 years his brother-in-law, Robert Southey, one of the most tirelessly-productive writers, formed the supportive centre of a household that comprised his own expanding family, the wife and three children abandoned by Coleridge, assorted aunts and countless cats. They called it 'the

Above: Greta Hall

ant hill' and it served as a home to all of them, as school to the children, work-place to Southey and a welcoming holiday refuge to many friends. The list of visitors amounts (almost) to a catalogue of the leading British writers of the time – William and Dorothy Wordsworth, Charles and Mary Lamb, William Hazlitt, Thomas De Quincey, the young poet Shelley and his new wife and Sir Walter Scott. They sketched each other and commissioned portraits; they described the house and its inmates and the surrounding countryside in long and vivid letters, many of which have survived.

The house itself has also survived, virtually unchanged in its external appearance. It is an imposing, solid looking, odd-shaped building. Faced in pale grey, it has a two-story frontage with rectangular sash windows and a Grecian-style front doorway with fluted Ionic columns supporting the pediment. On each side of the house, there is a single-storey semi-circular wing. It faces south-west, towards the Newlands Valley, and stands on a small hill top, above a great bend in the River Greta and close to the centre of the town. For all this, its encircling trees render Greta Hill all-but-invisible until you enter its garden. And for all the wealth of its connections, it is seldom visited.

It was built in the closing years of the 18th century by a local man, William Jackson, who had made his money in the coaching business. He was a bachelor and the house was far too big for his modest needs. So he was delighted, in the summer of 1800, when Coleridge moved in with his wife Sara and their son Hartley, almost four years old. Jackson gave them the larger and better part of his house and was so overwhelmed by Coleridge – almost everybody found the initial impact of his personality irresistible – that he wanted to let them have the place rent-free.

Coleridge came to the Lake District simply to be close to

Wordsworth, who had recently settled with his sister Dorothy at Dove Cottage in Grasmere. The three of them had already lived close together – "three persons with one soul" – by the shores of the Bristol Channel, striding about the Quantock hills, endlessly discussing politics and poetry, and writing poetry. This was the marvellous, inspirational year 1797-98 which saw the creation of the first edition of *The Lyrical Ballads*. For Wordsworth it was no more than a beginning; for Coleridge, as it turned out, it was the time when he wrote the poems for which he is now remembered, the *Ancient Mariner*, and the conversation piece, *Kubla Khan*.

The hope was that the joyful, creative companionship of two years before would now flourish again in Wordsworth's home county. Coleridge arrived in Keswick in July 1800 with a heavy cold and rheumatic fever. A less impetuous man might have wondered whether the Lake District climate was going to suit him. But as soon as he moved in , he bombarded his friends with excited letters, bubbling with high-spirited confidence, enthusing about the house and its immediate environs and most of all, the mountain views: *My dear fellow, I would that I could wrap up the view from my House in a pill of opium, and send it to you! I write to you from the Leads of Greta Hall, a Tenement in the possession of S.T.Coleridge Esq, Gentleman-Poet and Philosopher in a mist... my God! What a scene - right before me is a great Camp of single mountains – each in shape resembles a Giant's Tent ... the most fantastic mountains that ever Earthquakes made in sport; as fantastic as if Nature had laughed herself into the convulsion in which they were made...*

He was intoxicated with the place. In letter after letter he used the same image – the mountains of Newlands as a giants' encampment. He repeated another image too, describing his son's response to his new home: *Hartley is all Health and extasy – He is a spirit dancing on an aspen Leaf...*

Within three months there was another member of the family – *"Thanks,"* Coleridge said in a letter, *to my late Essay on Population!"* It was a boy and they called him Derwent, after the nearby river. Had it been a girl, she would have been called Greta.

Although he had pressing debts and no steady source of income, and though he was already beginning to fear the loss of his poetic power, Coleridge's spirits remained buoyant. He saw much of the Wordsworths. None of them thought anything of walking the 14 miles or so between their houses, talking for hours, then walking home again. Coleridge would make the journey at night, sometimes by way of Helvellyn summit. He wandered among the fells north of Keswick, and climbed Skiddaw and Carrock. Then he explored the Newlands area. He did not hire a guide, as others invariably did for trips in the higher mountains, he had no reliable map. He liked to get off the beaten tracks and make his own way, freely, up the fellsides and along the ridges. He was fascinated by the landscape and also by its influence on his feelings and thoughts and moods: *I must be alone,* he wrote, *if either my Imagination or heart are to be enriched.* Bad weather could not deter him; on the contrary, it was a stimulus. His letters and notebooks of this time are alive with the excitement of his mountain adventures and discoveries. He was the first true fell walker, doing it, not for any gain but purely for fun: *The farther I ascend from animated Nature, from men, and cattle, and the common birds of the woods and fields, the greater becomes in me the Intensity of the feeling of life.* In August 1802, looking for a shortcut from the summit of Scafell, he made the first recorded rock climb in England.

It sounds as if his three and a half years in Greta Hall was an idyllic period in Coleridge's life. In fact, it was climactic and disastrous.

As he had suspected, he could no longer write fine poetry. He struggled hard but he knew he failed. In some despair, he turned his attention to the more arid and complex studies of philosophy and science. And this at a time when Wordsworth was writing prolifically and growing, quite clearly, in poetic strength and range.

Coleridge's health, too, caused great trouble. Tramping the hills in all weathers did not help. Racked by rheumatism and neuralgia and a range of other afflictions, he relied increasingly on laudanum (a tincture of opium and alcohol) to alleviate the pains. Soon he was an addict. The necessary doses increased; he suffered frightful visions and nightmares; the sleeping house would be shaken by his cries. When he tried to reduce the dosage, he was subjected to horrific withdrawal symptoms. Always a close and acute observer of himself, he knew he was bound on a wheel that could shatter his life.

And his marriage collapsed. It must be doubted whether he and Sara were ever really compatible though their first years together seem to have been happy enough. It is doubtful indeed whether any woman – short of outright sainthood – could have tolerated for long the pressures imposed by Coleridge's demanding, unpredictable, unreliable, feckless and wayward temperament. By the summer of 1801 – when Coleridge had met and become infatuated with another woman, Sara Hutchinson – the strains on the marriage were serious. Before long, the peace of Greta Hall was frequently rent by their bitter quarrels and recriminations.

Coleridge spent more and more time away, then wrote a

series of letters urging the Southeys to come and share the house in Keswick with them. He hoped that the presence of others would make for a calmer, more controlled atmosphere. He also thought his wife might find comfort in the company of her sister Edith, who was Mrs Southey.

The Southeys, still mourning the death of their first child, moved into Greta Hall in September 1803. By the end of the year Coleridge had gone for good, seeking a kinder climate in the Mediterranean, leaving behind his wife and their two sons and a newly-born daughter, yet another Sara.

If Robert Southey felt fairly lumbered, he made no complaint. He was enraptured by the house and its environs and settled in to spend the rest of his life, another 40 years, there. Soon his own family began to appear, eight children in all, though only four survived to adulthood. The household also included another of Mrs Southey's sisters, Mary Lovell, a widow. And the owner of the house, William Jackson, was still in his quarters at the back, with his house-keeper. It was a full house, lively but orderly. Mrs Coleridge, who had a keen sense of fun and fantasy, said they lived *like bees in a hive.* They kept regular hours. The children went to different rooms for lessons: to Mrs Coleridge for writing and mathematics, French and Italian; Aunt Lovell for Latin and English; Southey himself for Spanish and Greek. But there was time, too, to run about the garden and along the river bank. When the weather allowed, there were family excursions and picnics, with much banter and joking. Letters of the period and subsequent memoirs describe a busy, bustling, noisy, animated, secure, hospitable and happy life.

At the centre of this teeming scene sat Robert Southey himself, sole bread-winner for them all. He had time for the children, at lessons or at play. He liked to walk for an hour or two

Samuel Taylor Coleridge   *Robert Southey*

each day. But most of his time was spent alone at his desk, surrounded by his beloved books, his pen moving ceaselessly across the white pages. A visitor in 1816 wrote: *Literature is now his trade... He is a manufacturer, and his workshop is his study.*

Unlike Coleridge, Southey was no original genius. Even more unlike Coleridge, he was conscientious, hard-working and entirely reliable. He wrote long letters every day to a wide range of friends; reviews and articles for the magazines; he edited and translated the works of others; he wrote hefty and worthy biographies and histories; and long epic poems which are hardly read today but which were very popular when they first appeared. He wrote shorter poems, too, and one or two of them still appear occasionally in anthologies. The best-known of his creations, though few remember that it was his, was the tale of *Goldilocks and the Three Bears.* In 1813 he was appointed Poet Laureate, after Walter Scott turned the offer down. Wordsworth had to wait a further 30 years, for Southey's death, before the honour came to him.

Southey never owned Greta Hall, he only rented it, and after his death the house had a succession of occupants, none of them particularly notable. For a few years it was a private school for girls. In 1909 Keswick School rented it to use as a boarding house. Twelve years later the governors of the school bought the place and ever since it has served as a boarding house for senior girls. The rooms where Coleridge and Southey and others talked and wrote are now dormitories, the walls plastered with posters of pop groups and other heroes of modern youth. Until recently the house held many mementoes of its distant, distinguished past – original letters and water colours and photographs were on display in the corridors. These were taken down some years ago and removed to Dove Cottage Museum to be restored and catalogued and properly preserved.

Today, Greta Hall holds few reminders of the great men who were there. Plaques on each side of the front entrance give the dates when Coleridge and Southey were in residence. In what they called *Southey's Parlour,* which was the family's dining and sitting room, there stands an elaborately-carved wooden cabinet which was presented to him by the Brazilian government in gratitude for his *History of Brazil.* On one wall you can see a collection of silhouettes of the family, made by an itinerant artist.

And that is all. It is all very different from what has been done at Wordsworth's main homes, the house in Cockermouth where he was born, Dove Cottage in Grasmere, and Rydal Mount where he died. They have been carefully restored, filled with appropriate things and made available to the public. They are major tourist attractions. Indeed, Dove Cottage, under the aegis of the Wordsworth Trust, has become the centre of a thriving minor industry with the cottage itself, a bookshop, a museum with a permanent exhibition and regular specialist exhibitions as well, a restaurant, and – for serious researchers – a library and a unique collection of manuscripts, pictures and books.

There is no call for a similar development at Greta Hall. The Dove Cottage complex covers Coleridge and Southey and others of the Lake circle quite adequately and it is best that all the material should be at the one centre. But it would be delightful if Greta Hall could be dedicated to its period of greatness, filled (as far as possible) with the things that were there nearly 200 years ago, and opened to the public. The chance to do this will arise soon. The governors of Keswick School have decided to concentrate the whole school, in future, on the Lairthwaite site, which presumably means that they will be selling the properties on the Keswick site, including Greta Hall. It would cost a lot of money, not just to buy the house but then to equip it to house old pictures and documents and furniture both safely and properly. But it would be a great thing for Keswick – and for Greta Hall – if it could be done.

Hall Caine

Fashion is every bit as fickle and tyrannical in literature as it is in women's clothing. In 50 years' time who will be reading the best-selling novelists of today – Jeffrey Archer and Catherine Cookson and Dick Francis? Probably nobody. Who today, except for a few poor academics who have to do it to keep their careers going, ever sits down to read the stories of Mrs. Humphrey Ward or Ouida or Harrison Ainsworth, all immensely popular in their day, in the early decades of this century?

Does anyone, simply for pleasure, ever turn to the long, melodramatic historical romances of Sir Thomas Henry Hall Caine, whose name dominated the best-seller lists from 1890 to 1914? Sic transit, as they used to say, gloria mundi.

Who was this Hall Caine? First and foremost, he was a remarkably successful storyteller, the writer of many stout and wordy volumes of costume drama, highly moralistic in tone and very much in tune with the public taste of his time. The stories were serialized in newspapers and magazines. In book form they sold by the hundreds of thousands. They were turned into stage plays and later into films. They won him a knighthood in 1919 and made him a Companion of Honour three years later.

He was also a character, small in stature but massive in ego and personality, flamboyant and eccentric in appearance, a great name-dropper and self-promoter, red haired and short-tempered and highly sensitive to criticism. Many people thought he resembled the portraits of Shakespeare and he took great pride in that. He lived for several years at a house on the

Hall Caine

eastern outskirts of Keswick, at the time when Canon Rawnsley was Vicar of Crosthwaite and a dynamic figure in Cumbrian life. Rawnsley wrote a book called "Literary Associations of the English Lakes," a big work in two fat volumes and strangely enough, it makes no mention at all of

Hall Caine, then at the height of his success and fame.

What could possibly be the reason for this?

Well, they were both men of powerful and assertive personalities. Perhaps Rawnsley simply could not stand the man? Or thought Caine's writing beneath his notice, not to be admitted to the company of such towering figures as Wordsworth and Coleridge.

Hall Caine was born in Runcorn, Cheshire in 1853, when Dickens and Thackeray were pushing the English novel to new heights of popularity. His father was a blacksmith, originally from the Isle of Man. His mother came from Whitehaven. He grew up in Liverpool and was apprenticed at the age of 14 to an architect. But he soon found that it was more fun and more lucrative to write pieces for the newspapers, first in Liverpool and then in the Isle of Man.

He developed an intense admiration for the famous painter and poet, Dante Gabriel Rossetti, founder of the Pre-Raphaelite Brotherhood of English painters. He wrote to Rossetti and was soon invited down to London to meet the great man. Immediately they took to each other, although Rossetti was twice Caine's age and an increasingly sick man, heavily addicted to the anaesthetic drug chloral. Caine became part of the Rossetti household in Cheyne Walk, Chelsea, acting as companion and nurse to his hero. In September 1881, he persuaded Rossetti to go up with him for a Lake District holiday, in the hope that it might improve his health. They stayed at Fisher Place, just north of Thirlmere, and on the first morning there, after a hearty breakfast, Rossetti proposed an ascent of the nearby little mountain Great Howe. He admired the view from the summit. "I am not one of those who care about scenery," he said, "but this is marvellous and the colour is wonderful."

On the way down, though, Rossetti lost his footing and slipped several yards through the bracken before Caine could stop him. He was concerned but Rossetti only laughed and said: "Don't be afraid. I always go up on my feet and come down on a broader basis."

Despite this moment of excitement and fun, the poet's health did not improve. He died a few months later, in Hall Caine's arms.

The Rossetti connection did much for Caine's career. He rapidly produced a book, "Recollections of Rossetti," which upset many of the poet's friends and relatives but helped to promote Caine's position in the journalistic world. Encouraged by this he started work on a long novel based on the Thirlmere region. It was called "Shadow of a Crime" and set in the time of Cromwell and the Restoration of the monarchy, a period of fierce religious and political divisions. To modern eyes , the books is impossibly hard going, turgid in style, high-sounding and pretentious and predictable, made even more painful by Caine's weird attempts at the Cumbrian dialect: "Shaf! He's bagged himself stump and rump," for example, whatever that may mean.

Grevel Lindop in his magisterial "Literary Guide," says the book "must rank as one of the worst novels ever written about the Lake District."

Even at that time, a century ago, the book did not sell. Soon after, however, Caine's writing career started to take off in a big way. A novel called "The Deemster" (The Manx name for a judge) sold very well in 1887 and was instantly adapted as a play which also proved a great success. Caine fancied himself as an actor and declaimer of his own stories, and greatly relished his growing connection with the world of theatre.

Then he came to live in Keswick, in a solid, four-square,

stone-built house on the edge of town on the Penrith Road. It was called "Hawthorns" in those days. The house is still there, known now as "Ash Tree House" in honour of the weeping ash in the front garden. The house itself looks much as it did a century ago, but the area around it is now considerably built-up. In Caine's day there were fields on three sides and a steep drop to the River Greta and wide open, extensive views to Latrigg and Skiddaw and across the roofs of Keswick to the Newlands Fells and Derwentwater.

In July 1892 a magazine journalist from London visited Caine at his Lakeland home, spent a few days there, and described his first-floor study, crammed with books and manuscripts and pictures and treasured mementos of Rossetti.

He also described Caine. "He is a son of the people, born of Manx and Cumbrian parents, and coming of the soil in a more literal sense perhaps than is the case with any other notable man of letters now living. The peasant and the student the man born to write books, and yet half fitted by nature for the life of the hills, a certain ruggedness of exterior (loosely, almost untidily dressed) with real delicacy of physique, the head of an Elizabethan, having a perfectly startling resemblance at some moments to the portraits of Shakespeare – it is certainly a curious and striking blend of personality."

Caine was a married man by this time. "The life that the mountain novelist lives up in the mountains," the journalist noted, "is a very simple one. That of his home circle quite primitive. Mrs. Caine is very energetic, and does her own milking, churning and cheese-making, for there is a cow, as well as a horse and all the other belongings of a country homestead."

In 1895 Caine went back to the Isle of Man to live there for the rest of his life. More novels poured from his prolific pen, most of them successful. He became popular as a lecturer too, Bohemian in dress and histrionic in performance. He was an enthusiastic traveller, paying long visits to Russia in 1892, the United States three years later, to Egypt and the Sudan in 1908.

Just before the outbreak of World War 1 his novel "The Woman thou gavest me" caused a great furore by attacking the stern, conventional attitudes of the time towards marriage and divorce and illegitimacy.

When war broke out he hurled himself into the propaganda effort, writing patriotic pieces for the newspapers, a play called "The Iron Hand," and even a film for the National War Aims Committee. The knighthood he got in 1919 was, in part at least, an acknowledgement of that war work.

He went on writing through the 1920's though he was over 70 by this time and his style and attitudes had already dropped hopelessly out of fashion. He died in the Isle of Man in 1931.

FOOTNOTE: *I began this article by doubting whether there was anyone today who reads Hall Caine's books. There is certainly one person who has read them all, a lady called Vivien Allen who lives in the Isle of Man and has been working for the past five years or so on Caine's biography. She is fascinated by the man, though by no means blind to the shortcomings of his character and writing style. "For today's taste," she wrote a few years ago, "Hall Caine over-eggs the omelette and bits are cringe-makingly sentimental." If all goes well her book will be published in the spring of next year.*

John Ruskin: Brantwood

When John Ruskin agreed to pay £1,500 for Brantwood, he had not seen the house. But he knew where it stood, above the eastern shore of Coniston Water. He also knew that it commanded wide and handsome views across the lake to the massy hump of Coniston Old Man and the village in the valley and more rugged mountain shapes to the north and the gentler, greener hills to the south. That was what he wanted – the position and the prospect – and when he went to inspect his newly

Above: Ruskin at Brantwood by W G Collingwood.
Opposite: Brantwood from Coniston by W J Linton.

acquired property in September 1871, although the building itself clearly needed attention, he was far from disappointed.

He wrote to his friend Charles Norton: *I've had a lovely day. The view from the house is finer than I expected, the house itself is dilapidated and rather dismal...a small place here, with five acres of rock and moor, a streamlet, and I think on the whole the finest view I know in Cumberland or Lancashire, with the sunset visible. Here I have rocks, streams, fresh air, and, for the first time in my life, the rest of the purposed home.*

He was looking for a sanctuary. He had known and loved the Lake District from childhood. It was here that his penetrating eyes were first opened to the grandeur of mountain landscape and the detailed, intricate beauties to be found in tiny plants and ferns, in lichen and in the rocks. So now, in his early fifties, coming to Brantwood and planning what he would do to adapt the house to his needs was like coming home.

He was full of hope and hurled himself, with characteristic wholeheartedness into the work. Extensive repairs were made. Onto his bedroom he had a turret built where he could stand and survey a vast panorama of mountains and lake. Later he added a spacious dining room with seven lancet windows. He crammed the place with his collections – rock specimens, shells, books and manuscripts, drawings and paintings.

"More treasures," he wrote, "than I could ever use in 50 years."

He had no time for trendy notions of décor and good taste: "It might look like a harlequin's jacket," he said of Brantwood, "for aught I care." But he filled it with objects that he found either fascinating or beautiful – or both. He designed his own wallpaper, then covered the walls with so many pictures that the paper could hardly be seen. In the grounds he had a lodge and a coach-house built and paths laid through the woods.

It could have been an idyllic retreat for such a man, a place where he might escape from time to time from the pressures of the world and his own driving sense of mission, to relax among his treasures and the quiet, natural surroundings that had entranced him all his life. It should have been so but it was not to be.

Ruskin was able to enjoy Brantwood for no more than five or six years and even during that period he was away more often than he was there. He still had his house in London. He had rooms too, in Oxford where he had to do much lecturing as the Slade Professor of Fine Art. And there were months of travel, around Britain, in the Alps, studying the paintings and architecture of Italy.

He was rich and famous and very busy. There were many men of outstanding vigour and confidence in Britain at that time but even in that company John Ruskin was an acknowledged giant. He had made his name as the champion of the later paintings of Turner, then as champion of the new school of Pre-Raphaelite painters. He was a prophet of natural beauty and mountain landscape. Later he used his incomparable powers of eloquence, in speech and in writing, to proclaim the glories of the Italian Renaissance painting and of European architecture, Gothic and Romanesque. At the age of 40 or so, he launched himself into a moral crusade (almost single-handed) against the evils of the new industrial society, where the few grew ever wealthier and the many lived as slaves to machinery. He fought the good fight with deeds as well as words, pouring his money and energies into his Guild of St. George whose aim was to restore to the workers a sense of craftsmanship and the dignity of independence.

All these causes demanded, and got, his passionate dedication. It is hardly surprising that, within five years of acquiring Brantwood, he was describing himself as "overwhelmed with the quantity of things which must be kept in my mind."

In early 1878, sitting at his desk in Brantwood, he wrote: *Morning breaks as I write, among these Coniston Fells, and the level mists, motionless, and grey beneath the rose of the moorlands, veil the lower woods, and the sleeping village, and the long lawns by the lake shore. Oh, that some one had but told me in my youth, when all my heart seemed to be set on these colours and clouds, that appear for a little while then vanish away, how little my love for them would serve me, when the silence of the lawn and wood in the dews of the morning should be completed: and all my thoughts should be of those whom, by neither, I was to meet more!*

Disillusioned and confused, he was beginning to fear for his sanity and the fear was well-founded. Before the year was out his hyper-active mind cracked and for weeks he was raving mad, convinced that the Devil was about to seize him.

In the years that followed the attacks grew more frequent and more intense. His cousin Joan, together with her husband Arthur Severn, managed the house and estate for him and nursed the old man through those last, long, terrible years. In his lucid periods he wrote his autobiography, '*Praeterita,*' the only book of his that is much read nowadays. But after 1889 he wrote virtually nothing and hardly spoke. For 11 years, until his death in 1900, the man who had been uniquely eloquent, whose words had profoundly influenced men so disparate as Leo Tolstoy and Bernard Shaw, Mahatma Gandhi and Oscar Wilde, was absolutely silent, except when he was demented.

He bequeathed Brantwood to the Severns, stipulating only that they should open the house to the public on 30 consecutive days each year. They ignored that. They lived there and when they needed money, they sold some of his things. By 1932, when they were both dead and the house itself was sold, nearly all its contents had been dispersed.

Fortunately, the house was bought by a great admirer of Ruskin, John Howard Whitehouse, who wanted to make it a memorial to the great man. He traced many of the scattered treasures, bought them and restored them to their old home. The structure had been neglected and there was much work to be done, but in April 1934 Brantwood was, at last, opened to the public. A trust was later created to safeguard its future.

Even after that, though, it had a chequered history.

I cannot remember when I first visited Brantwood but it was probably in the early 1960's. For all the beautiful things on display and the fine views, it seemed cluttered and awkward, a dark and dispiriting place, almost as if the house were still infected with the brooding, broken soul of the mad old man. Many others have felt the same. Frank Singleton, in the early 1950s, described it as "this undistinguished conglomeration of a house. It is the ugliness of everything that assaults the senses, the utter absence everywhere of beauty of design in things like household appointments and furniture."

And Hunter Davies, performing his 'Walk around the Lakes' in 1978 received a frosty welcome when he came to Brantwood.

"It was February and out of season," he recalled. "But I had been told the house could be seen by appointment so I had rung up and arranged to be shown around. I knocked at the door of the lodge, as instructed, and it was opened by a tall, gaunt-looking man who glared at me suspiciously. 'I thought you were coming next week,' he said, closing the door again.''

This has all changed in the last few years.

In 1982 the Trust appointed a young man called Bruce Hanson to manage the house and the estate. Originally from Lancashire, he had done various jobs in the Lake District, simply because he liked living there. After school, he had studied social history and come across the name of John Ruskin and became interested in his ideas. So when the Brantwood job came up he applied and rather to his surprise, he got it.

He has transformed the place. It is full of treasures – pictures by Ruskin and his artist friends, furniture, books, rocks and shells and much else – but there is no sense of crowding or clutter. He had wallpaper made to Ruskin's original design – a bold pattern in blue and grey and red, on a plain white ground – and it now graces the study and the drawing room. The rooms where Ruskin lived and worked and slept and entertained his visitors and gazed out at the lake and the mountains, all feel spacious and elegant and, when the sunlight streams through the windows, positively sparkling. Perhaps for the first time in more than a century, Brantwood is cheerful and welcoming once again.

Bruce Hanson has a direct and unpretentious but enthusiastic manner. It has been more than six years hard labour for him, and the job is not completed yet, but he makes no secret of his delight. "The place is coming alive again. You can feel it happening. It's very exciting," he says.

In the period of his management the number of annual visitors has grown from 12,000 to 33,000. Now, for his work at Brantwood, Bruce Hanson has been put on the shortlist of ten nominees for the National Art Collections Awards for 1989. The awards are given to recognize outstanding contributions made to

the visual arts by people who are not themselves creative artists.
The presentations were made at the Savoy Hotel in London, on May 8, by the Prince of Wales, who has been known to use powerful quotations from John Ruskin to upbraid some of today's architects.

He did indeed receive a major award but, he has also won the main battle: Brantwood is alive and flourishing, perhaps more stylish and attractive (to modern eyes) than it was even in Ruskin's first heady and hopeful days there, certainly full of interest for Ruskin fans and reflecting something of the buoyant, fearless, questing spirit of the man.

John Wilson

The Lake District story is rich in eccentric, larger-than-life characters, none of them larger or more extraordinary than the man they called John Wilson, of Elleray. In the course of his life he was accorded other names and titles among them "The Wizard of the North," "Lord High Admiral of Windermere," "The Professor" and "Christopher North." On the day he was born, May 18, 1785, there must have been a long queue of good fairies bearing precious gifts. John Wilson grew up with an unfair abundance of desirable qualities: wealth, stunning good looks, great physical strength and vigour, a sharp intelligence, an easy fluency in speech and writing, confidence and charm and

Above: John Wilson
Opposite: Elleray

generosity of spirit, a bubbling love of fun and company, the ability to make friends with people of all kinds and classes.

He was a Scotsman in origin, the eldest son of a prosperous Paisley merchant. Learning came so readily to him that he was sent to Glasgow University when he was 12. He studied hard there, but also found ample time for fishing and shooting, boxing and athletics as well as singing and playing the flute, dancing and, before long, falling in love. He was reading widely too, and already writing poetry. When Wordsworth brought out the second edition of "The Lyrical Ballads," Wilson was one of the select few who recognized immediately that the world of literature had a new and original genius on its hands. At the age of 17 he sent Wordsworth a fan letter, the first he ever got, and was rewarded with a grateful and thoughtful reply.

The next year he moved on to Oxford, Magdalen College. He was the leading figure of the time, equally outstanding in his studies, in social life, and on the sportsfield. He won the Newdigate Prize for poetry. He leapt 23 feet across the River Cherwell without getting his shoes wet, and ran the 57 miles from Oxford to London in eight and a half hours. His final examination papers were so impressive the examiners sent for him so that they might express their admiration in public. "The most illustrious examination within the memory of man," they said.

By this time Wilson was a Lake District land owner. On his travels he had been so struck by the Lakeland landscape and by the lively society of writers and artists that was gathering there, that he bought, while still a student at Oxford, several acres of land on the slopes of Orrest Head, above the north-eastern shores of Windermere. The region was known, as it still is, as Elleray. When John Wilson went to live there in 1807 there was nothing but a modest cottage, built in local stone in the mid-17th century and a superb view across the lake to the unmistakeable, craggy tops of the Langdale Pikes and the host of mountains ranging away to either side. Since then the railway has arrived and, following that, the crowded town of Windermere. Although the cottage still stands in green seclusion most of the Elleray area is now noisy with tourists and traffic.

John Wilson was young and rich and bursting with vigour. He hurled himself into the Lake District life at all levels. Thomas De Quincey, who became his closest friend, first saw him at a dance at Low Brathay, Ambleside, and could recall the scene vividly more than 20 years later:

At some of these dances it was that I first saw Wilson of Elleray, in circumstance of animation, and buoyant with youthful spirits, under the excitement of lights, wine, and above all, of female company. He, by the way, was the best male dancer (not professional) I have ever seen..... Here also danced the future wife of Professor Wilson, Miss Jane Penny, at that time the leading belle of the Lake Country.

De Quincey rapidly discovered that his friend was equally at home at Allan Bank in Grasmere, discussing poetry or politics or some other weighty matter with Wordsworth and Coleridge. He was at home too, and frequently at play, with the farmers and shepherds, huntsmen and publicans of Westmorland and Cumberland. His politics were high Tory, but in social life he was the complete democrat, striding cheerfully over the obtrusive class barriers of the time, judging people according to their characters, not their incomes or station in society. No one spanned the whole range of Lake District life as Wilson did.

He often walked over to Wasdale Head to carouse with "Owd Will Ritson" and his cronies. They fished the lake and swam in it, drank and talked the nights through in the Huntsmen's

Inn and held strenuous sporting contests. Ritson had been a champion wrestler, Cumberland and Westmorland style, but this did not deter Wilson from challenging him. Ritson won, throwing him twice out of three falls, but admitted that the professor was "a varra bad un to lick." When it came to jumping, Wilson was the winner, clearing 12 yards in three leaps while carrying a heavy stone in each hand. Ritson loved the man: "It was a' life an murth amang us as lang as Professor Wilson was at Wasd'le Head," he said.

Wilson loved organizing parties and expeditions for his friends. In 1809 he took 32 men including Wordsworth and De Quincey, with 12 ponies to carry camping gear and provisions, on a week-long angling trip. They crossed Wrynose and Hardknott passes, fished the Esk, then walked over to Wastwater for a few days' fishing there. He was an enthusiast for all country sports, particularly cock-fighting. He bred and reared his own birds, backed them heavily and supported them vociferously in the ring. He even had the dining room floor laid with turf so that he and his companions might enjoy "the mains" without the inconvenience of having to leave the house.

Wordsworth spoke of "Wilson and his merry men." Sister Dorothy, more disapprovingly, of "those wild companions of his." Wilson was the wildest of them all. He liked excitement and adventure and practical jokes. He once, it is said, crept into the dark room of the inn at Wythburn, where Wordsworth, Coleridge and De Quincey were waiting for a servant to bring them a lamp, and discharged a shotgun up the chimney, making them all jump and covering them with soot.

Money was no problem. He brought skilled craftsmen from Whitehaven and lodged them at the most expensive hotel in Bowness while they built him a fleet of boats – seven yachts, a ten-oared barge and many lighter craft. Then he had to employ boatmen to man the fleet. It made him the unchallenged "Lord High Admiral of Windermere."

He developed his property at Elleray. The barn at the eastern end of his cottage was converted to make a light and spacious drawing room with two tall windows. Then he designed and built a larger house, on the site that is now occupied by St Anne's Junior School. This has been completely replaced, but the house that Wilson built was, by all accounts, a rambling and eccentric place, forming three sides of a square and most of it single-storey. "I abhor stairs, he said, "and there can be no peace in any mansion where heavy footsteps may be heard overhead."

Occasionally friends would stay in the house but John Wilson preferred to live in the cottage higher up the hill. He never tired of the view. "Windermere seen at sunset from the spot where we now stand is at this moment the most beautiful scene on this earth," he wrote. There was also a special place in his heart for the sycamore that grew in front of the cottage. "Never in this well-wooded world, not even in the days of the Druids, could there be such another tree! It would be easier to suppose two Shakespeares. Oh, the sweetest and shadiest of all sycamores, we love thee beyond all other trees!"

It was an active life but he found time to write verse. In 1810 a volume was published, strange, dreamy, over-sentimental stuff that today's readers would be unable to stomach, but reasonably well-received at the time. The next year he married Jane Penny. They made a superbly handsome couple at the wedding and a very happy couple after it. They had two sons and three daughters.

This Lakeland idyll came to an abrupt end in 1814 when Wilson's entire fortune was lost through the dishonesty of an uncle who had been steward of the estate. Now it was time for Wilson to show the more sterling side of his character and he did. He had been studying law and now, with some financial help from De Quincey, he transferred his family to Edinburgh, hoping to employ his natural eloquence to restore his fortunes at the bar.

Very soon, however, he found that he could make more money and have a lot more fun as a journalist. He became a regular contributor to the Tory 'Blackwood's Magazine.' Before long he was a well-known figure in the city. Under the pen-name "Christopher North" he composed vitriolic attacks on the magazine's political and literary enemies and also, in marked contrast, soft-centered rhapsodies on the joys of life in the country. Later he turned his hand to long conversation pieces about a group of contrasting friends who discuss, in a discursive manner, everything under the sun. The writing came easily to him and proved popular.

In 1820 the Professorship of Moral Philosophy at Edinburgh University became vacant and Wilson saw no reason why he should not apply for it. The fact that he knew nothing whatever about moral philosophy did not deter him at all. He could always mug the subject up if he got the job. And there were two good reasons why he should apply. He needed the money, and he knew that the appointment would be made on party political grounds and that his party, the Tories, had a safe majority on the City Council which made the choice.

His rival candidate was an eminent moral philosopher but this counted for nothing when the vote was taken. Wilson was given the job by 21 votes to nine. Now he was "The Professor," too. He was delighted by the victory but perturbed as well because now he had to deliver a long series of lectures, virtually in public, and not only had no knowledge of the subject but also had nothing much to say. His friends, including De Quincey, were called in to help by suggesting lines of approach and actually writing many pages of the lectures. The whole story is disgraceful, of course, but there was nothing unusual about it in those days and, in the wayward way of such things, the appointment proved successful, even admirable. There was not much knowledge or logical thought in Wilson's lectures, but there was great eloquence and panache. They were not lessons so much as performances. The big man, usually very scruffy in costume, odd in behaviour, would appear before them with a mass of notes and then hold forth magnificently, full of confidence and character. It was not informative, perhaps, but it was vastly entertaining and sometimes stimulating to the minds and imaginations of his auditors.

Among his students was the young Thomas Carlyle, the future historian, who remembered Wilson many years later as a sort of human volcano: "Wilson, I suppose, never taught or much tried to teach; but he was a most eloquent, fervid, over-powering kind of man, alive to all high interests and noble objects. He stood erect like a tower; cloudy energy, determination, and even sincerity (or the visible wish to be sincere) looking out from every feature of him; giving you, among the chaos of his papers there, assurance of a man."

John Wilson's home for the rest of his life was in Edinburgh, in one of those handsome Georgian terraces. But he had not sold the Elleray estate and he and the family were often there, especially in the summer holidays. He kept his fleet on, too, and liked to take the commanding role in the regattas. The grandest occasion was in August 1825 when George Canning, Britain's Foreign Secretary, paid a visit to the Lake District. Everybody who was anybody was there – Wordsworth, naturally, the Poet Laureate Robert Southey from Keswick, the great novelist Sir Walter Scott, and John Wilson to organize the celebratory regatta. The local paper described an impressive procession of boats "accompanied by the roar of canon, the sound of bells, and the harmonious strains of two bands of music, while the shores re-echoed with the noise of cannon or the swelling note of the sonorous trumpet." Scott's friend and biographer, J. G. Lockhart, wrote: "The weather was as Elysian as the scenary . There were brilliant cavalcades through the woods in the mornings, and delicious boatings on the lake by moonlight; and the last day 'The Admiral of the Lake' presided over one of the most splendid regattas that ever enlivened Windermere. Perhaps there were not fewer than fifty barges following in the Professor's radiant procession..."

Wilson's wife died in 1837, and friends said this blow knocked much of the spirit out of him. But he went on working, writing his articles, delivering his philosophy lectures until he resigned the professorship in 1851. He died three years later.

It is not surprising that hardly anyone reads "Christopher North" today. Literary tastes have changed completely in a century and a half. It is not from what he wrote, but from what others wrote about him that we can get a vivid impression of the impact of his powerful, dazzling personality. The most moving tribute came from a most unlikely source, Harriet Martineau. She was an intellectual, strong-minded spinster. And she only encountered Wilson in his final declining years. Yet she wrote about him almost as if she had been in love with him: "Such a presence is rarely seen; and more than one person has said that he reminded him of the first man, Adam; so full was that large frame of vitality, force and sentience. His tread seemed almost to shake the streets, his eye almost saw through stone walls; and as for his voice, there was no heart that could stand before it. He swept away all hearts, withersoever he would…. Every old boatman and young angler, every hoary shepherd and primitive dame among the hills of the District, knew him and enjoyed his presence. He made others happy by being so intensely happy himself."

Mirehouse

There are few houses, even in the Lake District, that can claim to have a finer situation than Mirehouse. It stands near the eastern shore of Bassenthwaite Lake and some three miles north of Keswick, with the steep slopes of Dodd Wood and Ullock Pike to one side and green meadows leading gently down to the lakeside on the other. Although it is only a couple of hundred yards or so from the Keswick-Carlisle road, the sound of passing traffic is effectively baffled by woodland, notable for its venerable Scots pines. The house has a slightly faded air about

Above: Mirehouse

it. It is big but not imposing in any way, completely without pretension. It gives the impression of being entirely at ease – solid, durable and comfortable, perfectly contented to be exactly where it is.

For nearly ten years now it has been open to the public on two afternoons each week in the holiday season. The curious visitor can stroll round the main rooms, admiring their proportions and furnishings, studying a remarkable range and richness of mementoes of the days when the house was known to many remarkable men. There are letters from the pioneer geologist, Sir Charles Lyell; from John Stuart Mill and Matthew Arnold; from the fiery historian and prophet Thomas Carlyle and his first biographer, J.A. Froude; and from the brilliant translator, Edward FitzGerald. There are letters, too, and other mementoes of three successive Poets Laureate of the last century – Robert Southey, William Wordsworth and Alfred Lord Tennyson.

The central part of the house was built in 1666 as the headquarters for the Cumberland estates of the Earl of Derby. Before long it was the home of his agent in the country. At first it was a modest little house but towards the end of the 18th century it was made more impressive by the addition, at each end, of handsome canted bays. By this time it was the property of an elderly bachelor, Thomas Story, whose great friend was John Spedding, of Armathwaite Hall, at the northern end of the lake.

The Spedding family had made their money in and around Whitehaven, working as agents for the Lowthers during the boom years of the 18th century. This, and a judicious marriage, enabled them to buy the Armathwaite estate. John Spedding was born in 1770, the same year as Wordsworth (whose father was also an agent for the Lowthers), and for six years the boys were friends and fellow-pupils at Hawkshead Grammar School. The friendship lasted, though in later years it was chiefly maintained by the womenfolk of the families. John Spedding was a practical-minded countryman who saw little point in devoting your energies to the writing of poems.

The Speddings ran into severe financial difficulties in the last years of the 18th century. Armathwaite was costing more than they could afford. The young John Spedding had to miss university. He joined the army instead and went to the West Indies where he hoped to make enough money to rescue the family fortunes. It did not work out like that. When his parents died he returned home and found he had to sell the estate to meet his debts.

For a while he and his wife lived in Keswick. Then Thomas Story asked them to go and live with him at Mirehouse, which they gladly did because they had a son by this time. When Story died in 1802 he left the house and his vast estates to John Spedding, and they have belonged to successive generations of the Spedding family ever since.

John Spedding said his aim was to make Mirehouse "a thoroughly comfortable farmhouse, plentiful, hospitable, but no show." Over the years that followed there were extensions and alterations to the house but it was all done thoughtfully; no jarring or alien elements were introduced. It is because of this, and the care taken by his successors, that Mirehouse retains its settled, pleasant and harmonious air. Soon it was a very lively place. The Speddings had four sons and three daughters. The girls, who were by all accounts delightful, were educated at home. The boys went away to school and then to university. It was at school at Bury St. Edmunds that the third son, James, made friends with a clever contemporary called Edward FitzGerald. A few years later, at Cambridge, he got to know a promising young poet called Tennyson who was already a very noticeable Bohemian figure, big and oddly dressed, with a great mane of hair and a fine leonine head, usually wreathed in tobacco smoke.

In the spring of 1835, at James' invitation, FitzGerald and Tennyson stayed many weeks at Mirehouse. Both were in their mid-20s. FitzGerald was interested in literature but in a relaxed, light-hearted way. He never claimed to be anything more than a dilettante and would have been astonished to know that his translation of the *Rubaiyat of Omar Khayyam* (published anonymously in 1859) was to become one of the best-known and best-loved poems in the English language. Tennyson, on the other hand, was full of poetic ambition. He had already published two slim volumes and won prizes. Indeed, he paid for the trip to Mirehouse by selling the Gold Medal for English Verse, which he had won at Cambridge, for £15. They arrived in early April, which many believe to be the loveliest time of the year, when the meadows around Mirehouse are alive with daffodils. If the weather was fine the young men would stroll about the parkland, along the woodland paths and the lakeshore, talking endlessly. When it rained they settled themselves in the well-stocked library. FitzGerald –Old Fitz as they called him – would read a book. James Spedding drew sketches of his friends. Tennyson, meanwhile was at work. He was working on several poems at the time, among them *Morte d'Arthur,* the powerful narrative of the legendary king, his wounding and death and the returning of his magic sword *Excalibur* to the depths of the lake. It is generally agreed that many of the images in the poem were inspired by the scenes around Mirehouse, such lines as:

I heard the ripple washing in the reeds,
And the wild water lapping on the crag.

In 1974 when the Tennyson Society set up a stone

memorial lecturn by the lakeside, they had it engraved with the famous passage which describes how the arm rose from the lake, *Clothed in white samite, mystic, wonderful,* to catch the sword.

In the evenings, while FitzGerald played chess with Mrs Spedding, Tennyson and James withdrew to the Smoking Room, where through clouds of tobacco smoke, they would meticulously scrutinize Tennyson's work-in-progress. The master of the house, John Spedding, thought this a complete waste of energy. But he was too polite to do more than hint at his feelings.

The young men were having a marvellous time. They sat up till all hours, gossiping, discussing politics, reading Wordsworth's poems aloud. They had a high regard for Wordsworth's best work but were not blind to the shortcomings of his worst.

They held a contest to find out who could compose the weakest line in the most Wordsworthian manner, and FitzGerald claimed the victory with:

A Mr Wilkinson, a clergyman... For all the Bohemian flamboyance of his appearance and manner, Tennyson could be very shy. He resisted all James Spedding's suggestions that they should go over to Grasmere to see the great man. This was Tennyson's first visit to Mirehouse. His last took place 15 years later, in 1850, when he was on his honeymoon. Wordsworth had died early that year and Tennyson was soon to know that he had been appointed to succeed him as Poet Laureate.

Even more closely associated with the house and over a longer period, was another eminent and formidable man, Thomas Carlyle, historian and critic and thinker, a man with a highly idiosyncratic but vivid style, much given to indignation and fearlessly outspoken. He frightened some people and offended more. But his restless, prickly spirit always seems to have found refreshment and peace by the shores of Bassenthwaite Lake. He loved everything about Mirehouse, the place and its people. During the 1830s his home was in Dumfriesshire and he often journeyed to London, and he fell into the habit of breaking his journey to spend a few days at Mirehouse. His great friend there was the eldest son, Thomas. "The only man who really understands me," he said. It was there in 1848 that he was introduced to a nephew of the Speddings', James Anthony Froude, who was to become a distinguished historian himself and to write the first, highly controversial, biography of Carlyle. After a visit to Mirehouse in 1865 Carlyle described it in these words: "... everything nice and neat, dairy, cookery, lodging rooms. *Simplex munditis* (simple in its elegance) the real title of it, not to speak of Skiddaw, and the finest mountains of the earth."

Thomas Spedding had been trained in the law but now devoted most of his energies to helping his father with the running of the estate. The second son, John was away from home most of the time, a lawyer in Newcastle-upon-Tyne. It is from him that the present owner of Mirehouse, another John Spedding who also practices as a lawyer in Newcastle, is descended. The third brother was the literary and scholarly one. In 1837 James Spedding read a long, powerfully-argued article by Lord Macaulay in which he claimed that the Elizabethan statesman and philosopher Sir Francis Bacon, although undoubtedly a very clever and successful man, had been mean-spirited, materialistic and treacherously self-seeking. Spedding was so outraged by this judgement that he spent the best part of the next 40 years working to re-establish Bacon's good name. He studied all his writings. He collected early editions of his works, drafts of his speeches, original letters and accounts, the submissions he made to the House of Lords in 1621 when he was accused of corruption, and contemporary portraits of him. These treasures can be seen today in the Smoking Room at Mirehouse, together with James Spedding's monumental 14-volume *Letters and Life of Francis Bacon,* which was published between 1857 and 1874. Carlyle described the work as "the hugest and far the most faithful bit of literary navvywork I have ever met with in this generation." To his everlasting credit, James Spedding would have nothing to do with the dotty but very popular theory (at that time) that Bacon, in the midst of a busy and productive life, found enough surplus energy to knock off the plays attributed to Shakespeare in his spare time and in secret. Mirehouse has all this and much more besides. Among the letters on display is one from Robert Southey which suggests that Keswick was as much a prey to drunken vandalism two centuries ago as it is today. The letter is dated 27th March 1811. Southey calls on John Spedding to join with him in summoning a meeting of local worthies to discuss "measure for putting some check to the outrages which almost every night are committed in the town of Keswick." One of the outhouses of his home had been vandalized. It was not the first time it had happened. And Southey adds: "One main cause of the evil lies in the publicans, who keep their houses open much later than they should be suffered to do."

Thomas de Quincey: Nab Cottage

On March 13th, 1802, William Wordsworth and his sister Dorothy walked from their home at Town End (now called Dove Cottage) in Grasmere to see if there were any letters for them at Rydal. Dorothy wrote in her journal: *...It was terribly cold – we had two or three brisk hail showers. The hail stones looked clean and pretty upon the dry clean road. Little Peggy Simpson was standing at the door catching the hail stones in her hand. She grows very like her mother...* Margaret (Peggy) Simpson was six

Above: Nab Cottage

years old, the daughter of the man who farmed at what was then known as The Nab and is now called Nab Cottage.

The porch from which she reached out to catch the hail stones is still there. In fact, the whole south-facing front of the house, slate-roofed and white-plastered, with pointed stone-mullioned windows upstairs, a black lozenge-shaped date-stone above the porch, and one of those fat round chimneys that Wordsworth loved, looks much as it must have done in 1802.

The chief change is that in those days The Nab stood by the road side. Today a drive (the old carriage road) and a narrow strip of garden separate Nab Cottage from the A591, the main motor road through the heart of the Lake District. Across the road a gentle slope leads down to the reedy shoreline of the lake, beyond whose dark and sparkling waters stands the broad, hummocky mass of Loughrigg Fell. Behind the house the wooded ground rises steeply to the craggy summit ridge of Nab Scar. It is a splendid, varied, sun-soaking situation. Now the peace of the place is disturbed by the continuous noise of traffic and the occasional, sudden, shattering roar of low-flying military aircraft. A century and a half ago it must have been a blissful as well as a beautiful spot.

The house played an important part in the lives of two fascinating men. Thomas de Quincey was to fall in love with Margaret Simpson and marry her and live (sometimes) at the house and to further complicate his already insoluble financial problems by trying to save The Nab for the Simpson family. Hartley Coleridge, son of the Wordsworths' great friend, S.T. Coleridge, was to live there for the last years of his life. The tiny room where Hartley died can still be seen, little changed except that the fireplace has been blocked off. And by the window of the front sitting room, built into the wall in the old Lakeland fashion,

Thomas de Quincey

stands a tall wooden cupboard/desk, where De Quincey must have sat through the long hours of many a dark night, thinking and writing and measuring out his opium drops.

It so happens that these two rode past The Nab in a carriage in early November 1807. De Quincey was 22, a student at Oxford, a tiny and very sensitive young man, a voracious and serious reader with a quick and quirky intelligence. He was among the very first to recognize the innovative strength of Wordsworth's poetry. Five years earlier he had sent a fan letter to his hero, the first that Wordsworth ever received. Twice he had journeyed north to introduce himself to the great man but each time he had lost his nerve at the last moment and turned back, once when he was within sight of Dove Cottage. Now, though, he was on his way to the longed-for meeting. He had met Coleridge in Bristol and made friends. Coleridge's wife and three children were about to ride back to their home in Keswick. De Quincey's offer to escort them was gratefully accepted and he kept the children entertained with his lively chatter on the four-day journey. Now they were almost home, past Ambleside and Rydal and The Nab. The carriage slowed down on the steep pull up White Moss Common and the eldest of the children, Hartley, who was eleven, jumped down to run ahead. De Quincey followed him. He saw the boy turn in at the cottage garden gate. His heart in his mouth, he followed: *I heard a step, a voice, and, like a flash of lightening, I saw the figure emerge of a tallish man, who held out his hand, and saluted me with most cordial expressions of welcome.*

This meeting determined the course of De Quincey's life.

Next summer, his Oxford period disastrously terminated, he was back in Grasmere and before long had made himself an indispensable element in the Wordsworth household. He gave tireless and patient assistance to Wordsworth over a political pamphlet he was writing. He helped Coleridge in preparing to launch a new magazine. He amused and charmed the women and was soon adored by the children. He made good friends in the area. In 1809 he moved, together with thousands of books, into Dove cottage, which the Wordsworth's had been obliged to leave because it was no longer big enough for their expanding family.

De Quincey's health was not good and his will power was never strong and in the years that followed he grew ever more addicted to opium, which he took in the liquid form of laudanum. Soon he was finding it hard to get up in the mornings; hard to do anything useful when he did get up; hardest of all to resist the craving for more laudanum when darkness fell. When he finally fell asleep, he had terrifying nightmares.

By 1814 he was a regular evening visitor to The Nab. There was never any doubt about the reason. Margaret Simpson, 18 by now, had grown up to become an attractive woman with the qualities that De Quincey found especially appealing – a sweet, caring nature, the face of a girl, and a full, womanly figure. Before the end of 1816 she had given birth to a boy. In February the next year they married.

By this time there was an open breach with the Wordsworths. They had deplored De Quincey's mounting dependence on opium and all its anti-social symptoms. They had seen the effect on Coleridge and hated to find another friend falling victim. Their concern is understandable, even creditable. But then they disapproved strongly of his liaison with Margaret. He was marrying, they thought, beneath him. For all Wordsworth's admiration of the sturdy qualities of the Lakeland yeoman farmer – a constant theme in his poetry – they felt De Quincey was marrying a social inferior, and an intellectual inferior too. *A stupid heavy girl,* Dorothy said in a letter, *reckoned a dunce at Grasmere School.* They condemned the match and snubbed the newly-wed couple conveniently forgetting that Wordsworth, as a young man, had got a French girl with child and omitted to marry her. The Wordsworth belief that the marriage would prove a disaster was not fulfilled. Margaret proved a loving and loyal and infinitely-supportive wife, as much a mother as a wife to De Quincey who needed all the support he could get as his addiction grew and the creditors closed in.

He studied law. He turned to journalism, editing *The Westmorland Gazette* for 17 months. Then they moved to Edinburgh, where he wrote articles for the magazines and suddenly found himself famous when *Confessions of an Opium-Eater* was published in 1821. His writings were in great demand after this but he could never produce enough work to pay off the debts and maintain a wife and the accumulating children. He spent many weeks in sanctuary in Holyrood where defaulting debtors were safe from seizure and imprisonment.

It is a tribute to De Quincey's unworldly generosity of spirit that he did not hesitate to ride to the rescue when his wife's parents ran into serious money trouble. Some of the land they had been farming was rented but they had not been able to pay the rent for 14 years. There had been legal actions and they had not been able to pay the costs awarded against them. By 1827 it looked as though the family would have to sell the place that had been their home and livelihood for centuries. De Quincey hurried to Grasmere – he still rented Dove Cottage – and arranged a complex mortgage. It saved the situation, but only temporarily.

Now he was the virtual owner of The Nab so he and his family – there were six children by this time – moved in. Reasonable relations were restored with the Wordsworths. De Quincey invited a friend to come and stay, offering: *A glorious El Dorado of milk and butter and cream cheeses; mountain lamb equal to the Welsh; char famous to the antipodes; trout and pike from the very lake within 25 feet of our door; bread such as you have never presumed to dream of, made of our own wheat; new potatoes of celestial earthiness and raciness which with us last to October; and finally milk, milk, milk, cream, cream (hear it, though benighted Londoner!) in which you must and shall bathe.*

The euphoria could not last. Freelance journalism was then – as it remains to this day – a chancy and comparatively unrewarding craft. He found himself quite unable to meet the mortgage repayments. In September 1833 The Nab was sold by auction at the Salutation Inn, Ambleside, and became part of Rydal Manor.

Seven years later a young farmer and his wife, William and Eleanor Richardson, took the place over and brought with them their friend and lodger, Hartley Coleridge.

Hartley had much in common with De Quincey. He too was a tiny, odd-looking figure, quirky and unpredictable in manner, a great reader, full of humour and sharp observation, quick to make friends, especially among children, hopeless in the practical management of his life. Where De Quincey abandoned himself to opium, Hartley's downfall was alcohol. At least, De Quincey had a loving family around him. Hartley's family had all moved away.

It is never easy to be the son of a generally acknowledged great man and things were not made any easier for the young Hartley when his father proclaimed him a prodigy. He was, undoubtedly, a highly gifted and imaginative boy. He did well in the classroom, took a degree at Merton College, Oxford, and was offered a fellowship by Oriel. He so upset the authorities there – by his drinking, his unreliability, his outspokenness – that he had to leave after one year.

From then on it was a drifting, directionless life. He taught for a while in Ambleside, later at Sedbergh. He wrote and published many poems and a few essays and articles, on literary subjects. Like his father, he was for ever forming grand plans, never performing them. Mostly he lived a vagabond sort of life in the central Lake District, drinking and entertaining people with his witty talk and unconventional attitudes. *Li'le Hartley* became an almost universal favourite. Even Wordsworth, although he strongly disapproved of much of his behaviour, loved the man. Many locals though thought Hartley was much the better poet – there were more laughs in his verses – and some were sure that Hartley had written Wordsworth's poems for him. When he died in January 1849, Wordsworth ordered that the body should be laid alongside Wordsworth family graves.

For a further half century The Nab was a working farm.

Since then, with extra rooms built on at the back, it has been a guest house. Now it is run by a young couple Tim and Liz Melling, partly as a guest house, and during the summer as a language school where foreigners can stay to learn English and absorb the atmosphere.

The Mellings are very aware and proud of the cottage's literary connections. The house, they say, has a cheerful, easy-going ambience which they attribute to Hartley's gentle and genial influence. Tim Melling, more unexpectedly, also says that sometimes when he is alone in the house, day or night, he senses a strongly erotic female presence. To whom, in the long history of the place, might that be attributed? None of the women of the house has ever sensed this, perhaps not surprisingly. But other men have. I don't think I have ever heard before, of a sexually-stimulating supernatural happening, a sexy spirit at large. But Nab Cottage, or The Nab, or the Knabbe as Hartley Coleridge sometimes spelt it, has a tradition of the unusual.

John Richardson - Nobbut Me

When I first got a home in the Lake District in the late 60's, I went one evening to the local pub, the Sun Inn, Bassenthwaite, and sipped a pint at the bar where I overheard the animated conversation of a group of locals. To my dismay, I found I could hardly understand a word they were saying. For some time, indeed I could not even make out what they were talking about. Words were being used that I had never even heard before, and even when they sounded vaguely familiar the vowel sounds were so outlandishly broadened and lengthened that I could not fit it all

Above: St John's in the Vale.

together and make any recognizable sense. They knew I was listening and perhaps exaggerated the sounds to further bewilder and baffle the stranger's ears.

One thing, at least is clear, the spoken dialect is alive and vigorous in Cumberland. In the teeth of all pressures to impose a uniform Standard English, in the classrooms and through radio and television, many Cumbrians, especially in the remoter regions perhaps, still converse among themselves in a language that bears little apparent relationship to the English you hear from the announcers and newsreaders of the B.B.C.

John Richardson's headstone in St John's in the Vale

Later on, after my arrival in the Lake District I came to know Mrs. Enid Wilson of Keswick, who had lived all her life in the area and knew it, I think, better than anyone else – its plant life, animal life and human life too. In the limpid, fortnightly 'Country Diaries' that she wrote for 'The Guardian' for nearly

40 years, she shared her observations and knowledge with her readers and also her relish for the Cumbrian 'mak o' toak'. In one of her articles she gave the dialect names for a woman who won't stop talking. Standard English offers only chatterbox. Cumbrians can choose between three-ha' penny rattle, blatherskite, and chitterwallit. She heard a farmer describe another as "a cheerful laal beggar, he shines like a closet door on a frosty morning."

There is a wit and vitality and vividness in such use of words, a directness and something of the gritty quality of life itself, that you rarely hear in the talk of those who may be highly educated but have renounced their dialect heritage. Standard English tends to induce a blandness and a dullness in the spoken word. Dialect, in contrast, encourages humour and imagination, quirkiness and character. It gives a special force and richness and variety to language. Many of the words of the Cumbrian dialect are not English at all in origin, but Scandinavian, derived from the Viking invaders who settled across the north of England more than 1000 years ago. They are short, hard, single-syllable words, with precise meanings. In 'Land of the Lakes' Melvyn Bragg gives something like 100 Cumbrian dialect words that are used to designate the many different ways we have of beating or hitting each other. Think of all those sharp little adjectives – slape for slippery, thrang for busy, brant for steep, and verbs like fash (trouble) and flaatch (coax). My own favourite – twine (whine) – is widely used as both adjective and verb.

"Theer she goes, twining on, the twined old...."

The 20th century poet, Norman Nicholson of Millom, another writer who was fascinated by the special Cumbrian sound, often gave readings of his own verse and usually included one dialect poem. Whenever I heard him, it was the same piece

– John Richardson's "It's Nobbut Me." It is a well-turned and cheerful narrative about the tentative approach of a very shy country suitor, said to have been based on Richardson's own style of courtship. Nicholson always read it with great relish, as a way of leading into his own brief but powerful poem 'Nobbut God.' He got the idea for this, he would explain, from the splendid opening sentence of the Yorkshire dialect translation of the Old Testament: "First on, there was nobbut God."

There was a lot of writing in the Cumbrian dialect in the latter part of the 18th Century and throughout the 19th, songs and stories and poems, sometimes in lyrical praise of the landscape and the seasons and natural life, often telling a simple country tale. Although none of these writers attained the heights of Robert Burns in the Scottish Lowlands or William Barnes, of Dorset, there is a consensus that the best of the Cumbrian dialect poets was John Richardson.

John Richardson lived all his life at St. John's-in-the-Vale, some three miles east of Keswick. He was born at Stone Cottage, Naddle, in 1817, left school early to become a waller and builder, helped in the building of the sturdy stone church and its adjoining schoolhouse, and later – though self-taught for the most part – worked as school-master there for 22 years. At the age of 24 he married a local girl, Grace Birkett of Wythburn, Thirlmere, and they had nine children. He died at Bridge House by the beck and immediately below the church in 1886. He is buried a yard or two from the east wall of the church.

It seems to have been a quiet, simple, busy and happy life. He must have had a lively and curious mind, for – in spite of leaving school early – he managed to get and hold the teaching job and it was no sinecure. The school rules, (you can read them in the church), required that he should work in the classroom for seven hours every week-day and attend the Sunday morning service.

"The Master" they go on, 'will be required to give instruction in the following branches: viz, The Sacred Scriptures, Reading, Writing, Arithmetic, Mathematics, Book-keeping, Land Surveying, Geography, History, English Grammar etc."

In the 1870's he published two little volumes under the title 'Cumberland Talk.' They offer dialect poems and stories, and – in Standard English – an essay on the local dialect which shows that he had read widely and thought deeply about the subject. "Any one," he said, "who imagines that dialect consists of nothing more than corruption of, and badly-spelt, English, makes a great mistake. The fact is, that the English dialects are much older than the English language as spoken at the present time, and so far from their being corruptions of, and departures from, the standard tongue, that tongue has in a great measure been derived from the dialects."

He praises dialect for its forcefulness and human honesty: "Fwok say what they mean, an' they mean what they say." He closely analyses the Cumbrian mode of speech, its grammar, vocabulary, sounds and spelling, and remarks on the considerable variations you meet when you move from valley to valley. And he argues, convincingly, that the quality and gentility of life had improved in his life-time. His predecessor poets, he says, gave the impression that no wedding party or merry neet was regarded as complete until there had been a free-for-all punch-up. There was also a great deal of cruelty to animals, bull-baiting, badger-baiting and cock-fighting.

His own writings were free from such "rude and riotous scenes," not because he was mealy-mouthed but because they simply did not happen any more.

"During the last sixty or seventy years there has been a complete transformation among the rural population of Cumberland, in their diet, dress and manners," he wrote, "Instead of the oatmeal porridge, oatmeal bread, salt beef, and home-brewed ale, which were then almost their sole living; wheat bread, tea, coffee, sugar, and other articles, which were then thought great luxuries, may be now found in the poorest cottage. Instead of the coarse Skiddaw-grey coats, and the linsey-woolsey gowns and petticoats, which were then universally worn by old and young; the finest broadcloths, merinos, alpacas, and even silks, are common in every dwelling."

Richardson concludes his essay on the Cumbrian dialect by saying that "if, as some think, it should eventually disappear, we may venture to predict that it will die a very slow and lingering death."

If he were to return today, more than a century on, he would, I think, be glad to see how well the dialect has weathered the mounting pressures for national conformity. Most of the children of the county today seem to be virtually bi-lingual, speaking a more or less Standard English in the more formal situations and the broadest of local dialect variants at all other times. If there is not so much dialect writing nowadays – PACE Rene Roberts etc – there is still a lot of dialect speaking.

It is sad that so little is known about John Richardson. None of his contemporaries left any account of him. No portrait of the man has survived. All we have are a few basic facts and the two slim volumes. Yet an impression emerges of a good, conscientious, intelligent, modest and sympathetic man, who cared greatly for the place where he lived and the folk he lived among.

Since his time the Thirlmere valley has been changed,

almost beyond recognition and certainly beyond recall, by the thirst of Manchester. But Richardson's home region, St John's-in-the-Vale, is much the same as it was in his day. The church he helped to build stands four-square where he set it, in the little pass on the northern side of High Rigg, looking across the valley to the soaring ridges of Blencathra. The graveyard is rather bigger now and the church school that he built and where he later taught several generations of children has disappeared into a youth centre for the Carlisle diocese.

Norman Nicholson

At the very beginning of the very last volume of poems that he published, *Sea to the West* (1981), Norman Nicholson quoted some lines of W.H. Auden: A poet's hope: to be like some valley cheese, local, but prized elsewhere. It could serve as Nicholson's epitaph. That was his hope and he achieved it. No writer has ever been more rooted in, concerned for, and attached to the one little place – in his case the town of Millom on the south-west coast of Cumbria. And he was certainly prized elsewhere. His poems and books are still widely read and highly regarded throughout Britain.

The poems, in particular, give delight in Holland and Germany and across North America and in many other countries. The Russians read him in translation. A student in Sicily is writing a thesis about his work. Most of his poems are about Millom or the area around his experiences there, his family and friends and acquaintances, the iron works and the quarries, the rock and the rivers and the wild flowers. But he had the gift of seeing the universal in the particular. Millom, for him, was the world's microcosm. His poems speak to many thousands who will never see the town but who, through reading him have a true and vivid picture of what the place and its people are like.

It is a most unlikely place to serve for poetic inspiration. Surrounded by industrial dereliction and blasted by the prevailing winds, Millom crouches between the sands of the Duddon estuary and the waters of the Irish Sea, with the sprawling hump of Black Combe to the north and the Lake District fells beyond.

Norman Nicholson

It has little history. It was created in the latter half of the last century when vast seams of haematite were found there. The town sprang up and the shafts plunged down and more than 28 million tons of some of the richest iron ore in the world were extracted and processed. At the end of the 1960's it all ended, even more suddenly than it had begun.

Norman Nicholson saw it all happen and chronicled it:

...The hum

And blare that for a hundred years
Drummed at the town's deaf ears
Now fills the air with the roar of its silence.

It was a busy and thriving town when he was born, in 1914, at 14, St. George's Terrace, a few yards from the town centre. The short row of shops and offices were all built in Cumberland blue slate. In the little front room of the house, his father, Joseph, ran a gentleman's outfitters shop, working long hours to make just enough money to maintain his family and take them for a weeks holiday each year, very proud of being his own boss. The story of his growing up there is told in Nicholson's book *Wednesday Early Closing,* a richly evocative account, full of his love for the place and its people (his father especially) but direct and sharp and clear-eyed, never sentimental.

Norman was the only child and he was just turned five when his mother died. His grandmother took charge. Some years later his father married again and the boy acquired another 'mother.' It was one of the constants of his life – and one of the things he had in common with William Wordsworth – that for the greater part of his life there was a devoted woman more than happy to look after him.

He was a bright boy and a quick learner, fond of reading and good with words. His father's second marriage hurled him into the lively and sociable world of the Methodists and he soon found he had a considerable talent for public recitation. He won prizes for his dramatic declamations of popular verse. He loved it. It was here that he first heard the saying *giving it Wigan,* which meant giving it everything you have got. He did just that.

To the end of his life he believed that the purpose of words coincided with a perverse fashion for writing in riddles. Many critics regarded incomprehensibility as a positive poetic virtue. But Nicholson was not a man to compromise on what he saw as essentials, and he went his own way.

He was obviously destined for university but when he was 16 he started to cough, and the cough would not go away. In the end a specialist diagnosed tuberculosis. He spent almost two years in a sanatorium in the New Forest, resting and reading, learning to love the music of Bach, exposed to the fresh air (however fresh it was) and making a study of the visiting birds, speaking in a whisper to protect his larynx. In his poem *The Whisperer* he described this strange, anxious, very quiet existence and how it strengthened his need to communicate, to find an audience. He recovered in the end, sufficiently to go home, but he was always physically frail after that, having to rest each day and be careful. His larynx recovered, too, but he was left with a throaty voice that was both distinctive and charming.

Later on in his life, when his reputation as a poet was

growing, he gave many public readings of his own works. They were, literally, wonderful. I have heard Dylan Thomas, John Betjeman, Seamus Heaney and many others reading their own poems, but never a one to compare with him. He made an impressive presence – a slight figure but a fine, strong face, bright twinkling eyes under bushy eyebrows, the whole surrounded by a mane of hair and copious side-whiskers which became snowy-white in his later years. His readings were a performance and he took them seriously. The old *giving it Wigan* spirit never left him. But there was nothing of the ham in his style of reading. His aim, as ever, was communication. He would introduce each poem briefly, often with a gentle humour. He loved to tell the story of two little Millom boys who stopped him in the street one day, looked up and asked him in all seriousness: "Are you William Wordsworth?" And when he read his poem it would be with absolute authority, slowly, calm and controlled, using intensity of tone rather than volume when he needed emphasis, seeking always to bring out his meaning with the utmost clarity and force.

Wednesday Early Closing ends with the 18-year-old Norman Nicholson returning to Millom after his illness. He had been away, in a completely different world, for a very long time. Millom seemed ugly and unreal and unfamiliar; even the accents were strange to him now: *I stood outside the shop, while my father fumbled with the keys, and stared up to the attic window, which, in preparation for my coming, had been turned into a casement, to give me more fresh air. I did not know what was going to happen; I did not know where I really belonged.*

Then he added another sentence, the last one in the book: *Forty years later, in that same attic room, I thank God for a lifetime spent in that same town.*

For the rest of his life, some 55 years, that house was to be his home and he would rarely leave the town, never for very long. Millom, he said, was "a place that seems to belong to me like an outer layer of clothing so that anywhere else I feel not properly dressed."

The first years after his return home cannot have been easy. He had to discipline himself to a strict regime to safeguard his health. He could not hope to get a job. There must have been many times when he felt himself an unfair burden on his uncomplaining father's resources. His prime interest was in literature, modern novels and plays and poetry – T.S. Eliot was his hero – but in Millom he was effectively cut off from the literary mainstream.

In 1937, however, he started attending a course on modern poetry being run by the Workers' Educational Association. He was grateful to the W.E.A. ever after. The meetings were soon a dialogue between Nicholson and the tutor. It extended his reading and stimulated him to try his hand at writing – prose at first, novels and magazine articles. Before long he was given his own course to run for the W.E.A., a series of 12 lectures on modern literature for which he was paid £12. It was the first money he ever earned.

The Second World War saw a great upsurge in cultural interest in this country. Nicholson was now trying his hand at poetry. His work began to appear in a magazine called *Modern Reading,* then in the Penguin *New Writing* series. By 1942 he was well enough regarded to be asked to edit the Penguin *Anthology of Modern Religious Verse,* which sold 50,000 copies. Next year a slim volume came out, offering the works of three young poets, one of them Norman Nicholson. The year after that he published a poetry book of his own, *Five Rivers.*

Since then four more volumes of new poetry have appeared

and a couple of selections of his work. He was never a fluent or prolific writer. Each of the volumes is slim. Most of the poems are short. He was often inspired by an odd remark he heard or an incident remembered from his past or some local event that set him thinking. He would turn the idea over and over in his mind, for weeks, sometimes for months, even for years. There was no hurry. The important thing was to get it as right as possible. He prided himself on his technical skill, each job well and carefully done. The poet, he said, was like a potter, a craftsman. But he also said: "I like to think that when I have finished a poem you can drop it on the floor and it won't break." Not something you would hear a potter say of his work.

In the early days he wrote everything in longhand, by fountain-pen, often while sitting up in his bed in the attic. But his handwriting was close to indecipherable, and he was finally prevailed upon, by the complaints of publishers and printers, to use a portable typewriter. He did his writing from 10 am to lunchtime. In the afternoons he would sleep a little and take a gentle walk. The evenings were for letter-writing and revision.

Soon after the end of the war he wrote a verse play in three acts, *The Old Man of the Mountains,* transferring the tale of Elijah and the raven to a Cumberland setting and proclaiming causes that would now be called environmental. There was a vogue for poetic drama at that time and the play was staged at the Mercury Theatre in London. Nicholson went down for the first night and was delighted and excited to find himself sitting next to no less a person than T.S. Eliot. He sat through the show in a turmoil of conflicting emotions – of pride, anxiety, apprehension and mounting curiosity about what the great man's reactions would be. But Eliot was a man of austere manner and taciturn. Throughout the performance he hardly moved and made no comment at all. As they shuffled out at the end, Nicholson was relieved to hear the judgement: "Promising, Nicholson. Very promising." Nicholson wrote three more verse dramas in the 1950's but none of them was a great success. He also wrote several topographical books, describing the landscape and geology and history of the counties of Cumberland and Westmorland (as they were then called). And did a great deal of journalism in his later years, all of it carefully researched and written. But there is no doubt that it is for his poetry that he will be remembered by future generations.

Once he started publishing poetry, the recognition quickly came. His very first solo volume won the Heinemann Prize in 1944. Ten years later *The Pot Geranium* was the first recommendation of the newly-formed Poetry Book Society. Several universities gave him honorary degrees. In 1977 he received the Queen's Gold Medal Award for poetry. When the Poet Laureate John Betjeman died there were many who thought that Nicholson would make a very worthy successor.

He was by this time a happily married man. Yvonne Gardner was an English teacher at a local girls' school and very keen on drama. She decided to produce one of his verse plays and went to him for advice. They fell in love and, though there were no children, lived in close and harmonious partnership for more than 25 years. She looked after him, protected him from over-demanding admirers, drove him to his appointments and engagements, and read his poems almost as well as he did.

There were fears that he would not recover from her death in 1982, but he was a man of great inner resource and strength. In his last few years, though he was writing little by this time, his readings seemed to acquire an even deeper and more compelling authority. Peggy Troll, who had been a colleague of

Yvonne's at the school and had become a close family friend, now became his particular friend.

The year 1984 was a triumphant one for him. It was his 70th birthday that year and his friend and fellow-poet, Bill Scammell of Cockermouth, edited a collection of poems, specially written by many of the leading poets of the day to celebrate the occasion. Nicholson was moved and delighted. This was the year, too, when Lancaster University made him an honorary Doctor of Letters. And best of all from his point of view, he won acclaim from his home town. He was the first person to be made a Freeman of the Borough of Copeland.

He had been something of a venerable local worthy for some time – opening the new book shop in Millom and the Folk Museum and that sort of thing – and now he was a celebrity. But he did not behave like one. He went on, very simply, being himself – living quietly, without pretention or ostentation. He still lived in the house where he had been born and he had hardly changed it, except to make the first-floor front room his library, holding thousands of books. The shelves upon which his father had kept stock neatly ranged were still there. He liked the old familiar things around him, reminding him of the many years he had spent there.

Some Millom folk thought of him as a recluse. Each day he would walk the streets of the town in his coat and flat cap, his head bowed and his mind far away, working on some problem in his current writing. It was easily mistaken for standoffishness. Nicholson was a shy and very private man, never afraid to speak his mind but neither a club man nor a pub man. Beneath the shyness, though, there was friendliness, frankness and generosity of spirit. He was a good listener as well as a lively talker, often funny. He liked to take a glass or two of malt whisky in the evenings with friends. He was fond of watching snooker and cricket on the television. He loved to play the music of favourite composers – Haydn and Mozart, Bach, the late Beethoven quartets. He gave advice and encouragement to many young writers, among them Bill Scammell, Melvyn Bragg and Irvine Hunt who became a very close friend and, when Nicholson died in May 1987, his literary executor.

It is inevitable, I suppose, that he should be compared with Wordsworth. Both were devoted to Cumbria. Each dedicated himself to writing poetry. Both wrote, mostly, about their home areas. In other ways, they were entirely different. Wordsworth's output was enormous and Nicholson's was not. If Nicholson never quite reached the sublime heights of Wordsworth at his best, neither did he ever fall to the depths of Wordsworth at his worst. Their aims and attitudes were very different, their styles, their tones of voice. Wordsworth was a supreme egotist, pompous and humourless, a rabid reactionary in his middle and later years. Norman Nicholson was not like that at all. Yet his poems, I believe, will be read (as Wordsworth's will) as long as there are people to read poetry. The first step to ensure that happens should be taken, promptly, by his publishers, Faber and Faber, by bringing out a volume of all his poems.

The house where Nicholson lived and worked is a health food shop now with a little café where his sitting room was. A plaque outside proclaims him *Man of Millom* which he would have liked very much. The people of the town remember him with respect and some pride, many with affection. The town council has launched a memorial fund, aiming to raise at least £25,000 to help young writers. The Folk Museum displays an interesting collection of his papers and relevant photographs. The main room of the public library is called the Norman Nicholson

Room and contains a handsome bronze of his head. A plaque beneath lists his honours and quotes from one of the poems of his later years in which he describes the great dazzle of light which sunset brings to the Millom coastline

Let my eyes at the last be blinded
Not by the dark
But by dazzle.

The Rev. William Spooner by Max Beerbohm

The Rev. William Spooner

It is given to very few people to bequeath their names to the enormous and rich vocabulary of the English language. The unpopular Irish landlord Captain Boycott was one of them. So were Charles Mackintosh who invented a form of waterproofing, and John Macadam who improved our road surfaces; the 4th Earl of Sandwich who wanted to go on gambling, so ordered himself cooked meat between two slices of bread; and Thomas Bowdler who spent years taking all the rude bits out of Shakespeare's plays, so that they might be read aloud in front of the children without impropriety.

Another was the Rev. William Spooner.

Above: How Foot, Grasmere.

He was born in Staffordshire in 1844, an albino boy with weak eyesight and near-white hair and something of a stammer. If he was physically disadvantaged, he was intellectually brilliant. At Oswestry Grammar School he won a scholarship to New College, Oxford. There he took a double first in Classics and was immediately made a Fellow of the college. He lectured in philosophy, took Holy Orders and became Dean of the college, then its Warden. He was still in command of the college when he died in 1930, having passed 63 years there without missing a single term. He was greatly respected as a scholar and loved for his kindheartedness and generosity.

Today he is remembered, with gratitude, for his invention of what is called the "Spoonerism," which simply means the transposing of two sounds within the same sentence or phrase. The first, and probably most famous example, occurred in New College chapel in 1879 when he announced the next hymn with the words: "Number One Seven Five – Kinkering Kongs their titles take."

Word soon got around and a new fashion was set. This was mid-Victorian England where puns and word games were much appreciated, and before long dozens of "Spoonerisms" were being passed round:

"Our Lord, we know, is a shoving leopard."

"All of us have in our hearts a half-warmed fish to lead a better life."

"You have tasted a whole worm. You have hissed my mystery lectures. You will leave by the town drain."

"A toast to the queer old Dean!"

On a walking holiday in Switzerland he applied himself to the study of the new science of geology, and on his return home told a friend: "We spent a long time in a most interesting valley, completely surrounded by erotic blacks."

The Rev. Spooner firmly denied that he had ever said any of these things. He was a good and truthful man and I feel sure that he was right. There was no harm in the jokes, and a lot of fun, and many of the brighter students and dons probably had a splendid time dreaming up ever dottier variations on the verbal theme.

Oxford loves eccentrics. It has provided a home and living to hundreds, and Spooner was certainly one of them and he grew more eccentric as he grew older. He became Warden of New College in 1903. Shortly afterwards, meeting a young don in the quadrangle, he said: "Do come to dinner tonight to meet our new Fellow, Casson."

"But my dear Warden, I am Casson."

"Never mind, come along all the same."

He often went to preach in the village churches around Oxford and on one occasion devoted the whole of his address, to everyone's surprise, to the thoughts of the Greek philosopher Aristotle. He had finished and was leaving the pulpit when something occurred to him and he climbed back up again and said: "Excuse me, dear brethren. I just want to say that in my sermon whenever I mentioned Aristotle I should have said St. Paul."

And one more story, if you can stand it – or even if you can't. In London, it is reported, he entered an optician's shop and asked for a "signifying glass." The man was bewildered, but Spooner reassured him: "Just an ordinary signifying glass."

"I'm afraid we haven't got one in stock sir, but we'll order one right away."

"Oh don't bother," Spooner said, "it doesn't magnify a

great deal."

All very well, you might say, but what has any of this to do with Cumbria? And why is it appearing in the pages of "Cumbria Life" magazine?

The questions are reasonable and relevant, and there are two good answers. The first is that Rev. William Spooner, like many of the eminent academics of the Victorian and Edwardian eras, was a frequent visitor to the Lake District and very fond of fell walking. His favourite area was that around Grasmere and Rydal. He had a holiday home at How Foot just above the Wordsworths' Dove Cottage – How Foot is now a hotel – and he is buried in Grasmere churchyard.

W.G. Collingwood

It is the secret ambition of every right-thinking man and woman to be described, by some discerning observer, as a "Renaissance figure," meaning some-one who lays claim to a high level of achievement in more than one, and preferably several, quite different fields of human endeavour. The prototypes are the great men of the Italian Renaissance – Michaelangelo who excelled as sculptor and painter and architect and was an accomplished poet as well and, even more remarkable an all-rounder, Leonardo da Vinci, a master of the visual arts in many media, gifted musician, a civil and military engineer, a leading and inventive thinker in many branches of science including natural history, anatomy, mechanics, geology and the

Above:Collingwood's house at Lanehead, Coniston.

141

theory of flight.

It is doubtful whether anyone has ever matched them, or ever will, for sheer quality and variety of achievement. Among the English, perhaps Sir Walter Raleigh, the Tudor explorer and poet and courtier, comes closest to the ideal; in this century, Sir Winston Churchill.

In the Cumbrian story one name springs most readily to mind, though it is not a name that you often come across nowadays –

W.G. Collingwood

unless, that is, you are a follower of the teachings of Dr William Rollinson, of Ulverston. For five years ago Bill Rollinson, as he is generally known, brought out a revised edition of W.G. Collingwood's classic book "The Lake Counties," and confessed in the introduction that the man from the past he would most liked to have met was William Gershom Collingwood.

Collingwood was born in Liverpool in 1854. There was a strong artistic tradition on his father's side of the family and it was not long before the boy was being taken on trips to Windermere, sketching and exploring the hills and valleys of the southern Lake District. They stayed at Gillhead on the eastern shore of the lake, usually with a local fisherman called William Alexander who would hold the boy spell-bound in the evenings with tales about the days when the Romans and Vikings roamed the fells. For the young Collingwood it was the beginning of a lifelong fascination. Later in life he recalled Alexander, with gratitude and some exaggeration, as "the only man who ever taught me anything."

He loved the Lake District from the first moment, much preferring it to Liverpool. In a letter home he said: "I am glad to be near fells again and have made a few trips to the heights. One gets the mountain feel with a wonderful swiftness after leaving Coniston behind. The stars are much brighter here than in Liverpool" One April day when he was 16 years old he made his own way alone, from Gillhead to the top of Coniston Old Man.

"Rowed across the lake," he wrote. "Icy. Then across Esthwaite Water to Hawkshead. Then I saw the Old Gentleman who was wearing a white hat and asserted his gentlemanly origin by pulling it off to me. I went past the copper mines and was soon out of reach of houses and such like abominations. There was a blue haze which spoilt the view from the top – but the near peaks were glorious. I refreshed myself with snow and by 12 of Greenwich time precisely I got up on the cairn and yelled 'hip hip hurrah' as I had promised. But the Gillhead people neither heard nor saw me."

With a quick, retentive mind and the capacity for intense concentration, he won his way to Oxford where he studied philosophy. He worked hard but found time to make the acquaintance and then the friendship of one of the great men of the university, John Ruskin, Slade Professor of the Fine Arts. This was to be another formative influence. Ruskin agreed to let Collingwood attend his drawing classes, scrutinized his efforts and offered criticism and advice. Collingwood was so talented, academically and artistically, that he had no clear notion what he was going to do with his life.

Ruskin reassured him. "He compared me to a compass needle. I would find some attraction one way or another." Collingwood wrote.

In the event Collingwood never had to make a definitive decision. He contrived for himself a way of life, simple and varied and always busy, that enabled him to give full rein to all his abilities and interests researching, writing, editing, painting and drawing, exploring the Lake District and its history, walking the fells and climbing the crags, sailing and swimming, creating around him a happy and creative circle of family and friends. His was an all-generous spirit. And he was really helped by the fact that he would not let himself be worried about money-making and material possessions. What mattered, he believed, was to make a good, thorough, craftsmanlike job of whatever you were doing, not how much money you might make. This may have been something he learned from Ruskin – it is certainly an important part of the Ruskin message. But the attitude seems to have come naturally to Collingwood, and it made for a very happy and fulfilled life and one that is a pleasure to contemplate in these post Thatcherite days when the accountants and their balance sheets have come to dominate so many aspects of our lives.

Collingwood got a First Class Honours degree at Oxford and moved to the Slade School in London to improve his skills as a painter. John Ruskin continued to keep a concerned eye on his progress, then invited him to go and stay at Brantwood, his splendid house on the shores of Lake Coniston. Collingwood spent most of the summer of 1875 there, doing some translations from the Greek for Ruskin and helping to dig out a harbour and build a pier for the Brantwood boat, "Jumping Jenny."

It was about this time that he met and fell in love with a

young art student from Essex, Edith Mary Isaac. There was family opposition to their marriage, on the grounds that he still showed no signs of ever being able to earn an adequate income. Fortunately, the young woman seems to have been as cheerfully unconcerned about this as Collingwood was. They married in 1883. They had already got themselves a cottage at Gillhead and in the next few years four children arrived, three girls and a boy called Robin. In 1891 they moved to Lanehead, a mile from Brantwood.

By this time Collingwood had made himself virtually indispensable to Ruskin and the old man's dependence grew as he became ever more cantankerous and odd. One of Collingwood's letters gives a sad but sympathetic picture of those years.

"I make no doubt that the continual grumbling and looking at the bad things and their incurableness has to some extent warped Mr. R's mind lately," he wrote, "Most people say he is mad. I know that on many points he is more sensible than most of us. He has lost faith in Christianity and one cannot tell how far. He declares he delights in puzzling people and he puzzles me. Mr. R is not very well; he has been dabbling in spiritualism again. He talks of seeing ghosts and getting news from the spiritual world."

In 1893 Collingwood published a two-volume "Life of John Ruskin," a carefully researched and pleasantly-written biography which contrives, in the manner of the period, to skate discreetly round the more dubious and controversial aspects of the subject. When Ruskin died in 1900, Collingwood designed the elaborate and heavily symbolic Anglican cross headstone, that marks the grave in Coniston churchyard.

The 1890s were a particularly productive time. The

Collingwoods were busily painting to make a little money, and educating their young children. He grew deeply interested in the pre-Norman history of the Lake District, excavating the remains of the Roman fort on Hardknott Pass, studying the Viking invasions and the links between the old Norse language and the dialect words and place names of Cumbria. He wrote several historical romances, the most successful of which was "Thorstein of the Mere," published in 1895. Collingwood wrote the tale, he said, for his five-year-old son Robin, who was already showing signs of a prodigious intelligence. It was meant to be "a picture of his home as it might have been, a thousand years ago." The book gives a lively, colourful and imaginative account (though based on deep learning) of the discovery of Thorstein of the lake which is today called Coniston Water but which used to be called Thurston Water.

This is the moment in the book, when the adventurous young man gets his first view of the lake: "Thorstein climbed a howe on the left; and as he climbed, the lake opened up before him. Beyond the nearer woods there was the deep of blue, and the lonely island in the midst of it; and from his feet, away into the uttermost distance, the huge fells, tossing like the breakers on a stormy beach, and rolling away and afar like the heaving waves of the sea. And over them late sunset brooded in the north, with bars of level cloud, purple and dun, and fading rose-flecks overhead."

In 1897 Collingwood went to Iceland to study the impact of the Norse culture there and work on a book "Pilgrimage to the Saga Steads of Iceland." It is still highly-regarded in Iceland. Indeed, Collingwood is much more widely and fondly remembered there, as historian and saga-teller and painter, than he is in his own country. The National Museum in Reykjavik has his collection of water-colours. As he sailed for home at the end of the trip he was delighted when the pilot assumed, from his bronzed and bearded appearance, that he must be the ship's skipper.

In 1902 he produced the book for which he is probably best-known in Britain today, "The Lake Counties," a comprehensive historical description of the whole region between the Pennines and the Irish Sea, from the Kent Valley in the south to the Roman Wall. A great deal has changed in Cumbria in the subsequent 90 years but the original book can still be read with pleasure and profit. For those who like their information more up-to-date, there is Dr Rollinson's revised edition of 1988.

He got a job as Professor of Fine Arts at University College, Reading, in 1905, but though he did the work conscientiously as always, his heart was in Cumbria. Just before the outbreak of the First World War he produced another work of formidable scholarship, "Elizabethan Keswick," the detailed story of the German miners who were brought over in the 16th century to launch two centuries of intensive mining in the fells of the Lake District. This book was published by the Cumberland and Westmorland Antiquarian and Archaeological Society. Collingwood had joined the Society in 1887. He was soon reading learned papers and publishing articles in their annual "Transactions." In 1900 he became editor of the "Transactions," later the society's president, and for nearly 30 years was the presiding and energizing spirit of the society, setting meticulous standards.

His last great work, "Northumbrian Crosses of the pre-Norman Age," which he illustrated as well as wrote, was published in 1927. He died five years later and his obituary in the

"Transactions" said: "In his life he was no less simple and abstemious than if he had been vowed to poverty, which in effect he was, for he regarded time spent in earning money as time wasted from worthier employments, and he always gave away whatever of value he possessed, as generously as he gave his time and his knowledge to all who asked for them. Hard work for him was never drudgery, so insatiable was his appetite for it, and his capacity for enjoyment never failed him."

Many writers have paid tribute to the life-enhancing influence of Collingwood and the very special ambience that he and his wife created at their home Lanehead. In 1902 their son Robin invited a schoolfriend to stay with them in the holidays. This was an Armenian boy called Ernest Altounyan who went to the Coniston house and was immediately enchanted. Many years later Ernest's daughter (who was Collingwood's grand daughter) wrote a charming book, "Chimes from a Wooden Bell," and described her father's delight as follows:

"A strong feeling of 'coming home' wrapped him round and remained with him all his life. Apart from not having to go to church there were many things that were wonderfully different about the Collingwood way of life. The family of six were all unlike anyone Ernest had ever met before. The special atmosphere of the house (the smell of oil paint the moment you were through the front door, the music before breakfast, the cheerful industry) was also new. Probably Ernest had never before heard so much serious talk about art. The Collingwoods did not care to spend money on furniture unless it was special hand-made furniture, and money was only important because it could leave you free to do what you wanted. From the moment he arrived, Ernest fell permanently in love with the house, its scenery and its inhabitants. He even quite liked rain when it was

Coniston rain"

The following summer another young man arrived on the Collingwood scene. His life, like Ernest Altounyan's was to be become totally embroiled with the Collingwood's and immeasurably enriched. He was an Englishman, aged 19, hoping to become a poet. He later described, in his autobiography, how he took a room in Coniston village, walked up by the Copper Mines Beck, then leapt across the torrent to settle on a big boulder with his notebook.

"It so happened that on that day Mr. W.G. Collingwood, Ruskin's biographer, had been painting a picture higher up the Old Man," he wrote in the diary. "Towards evening he was walking home and on coming to the bridge over the beck saw what he thought was a corpse washed up on that flat rock. He called out and was relieved when the corpse lifted its head. I got up and jumped ashore, because the noise of the rushing water was such that I could not hear what he was saying. He asked me what I was doing and I told him I had been trying to write poetry. Instead of laughing, he seemed to think it a reasonable occupation and we walked down to the village together. Before we parted he asked me to come round the head of the lake to see him."

He did go round to Lanehead and he, too, was promptly captivated by the whole family. For a while he was Ernest's unsuccessful rival for the hand of one of his daughters. Later still, it was Ernest's children, sailing on the lake and exploring the islands, that gave him the idea for an adventure story which he called "Swallows and Amazons." The young man was, of course, Arthur Ransome, an even more remarkable man (in some ways) than his hero and mentor, W.G. Collingwood.

William Shakespeare

There is no historical evidence at all that William Shakespeare ever visited the Lake District, or any other part of Cumbria for that matter. Nor are there any passages in any of the plays or poems that can reasonably be cited as evidence that he knew our northern fells and lakes. When he writes about valleys and mountains they are usually Italian rather than British and when he took the action of his plays to hilly or steep-sided regions of Britain it was not the north-west corner of England that he chose. The hills and woods and "blasted heaths" of *Macbeth,* for example, are Scottish; the kidnapped princes in *Cymbeline* ("Now for our mountain sport...") are abducted to wilderness areas of South Wales, the blinded Earl of Gloucester in *King Lear* makes his suicide bid, or thinks he does, from the top of the white cliffs of Dover, a place now known as Shakespeare's Cliff.

There is one direct reference to our region in one of the historical plays *Henry IV Part 1*. When Falstaff is lying outrageously about his midnight fight against highway thieves on Gad's Hill, he claims to have been suddenly attacked by, and to have summarily dealt with, "three misbegotten knaves in Kendal green." It is a nice touch but alas, it proves nothing. Kendal cloth, and its distinctive dye, were known all over the country. There is an Earl of Westmorland in that play, and another, earlier Earl of Westmorland in one of the other Henry plays, but these facts mean nothing either – in those days such titles often implied no close regional connection.

One of the reasons why so many scholars have written so much about Shakespeare – and the reason why so much of what they have written is pure surmise – is that documentary evidence about his life is hard to come by. The dates of his birth and death are known, and of his marriage to Anne Hathaway, and of the christenings of their three children. He was born in Stratford in 1564, married there in 1582, and died there in 1616. It is also known that by 1592 at the latest he was established in London in his career as an actor and a writer of plays. For the rest, especially in the years up to 1592, the historians are on uncertain ground, and not at all helped by Shakespeare's careless way of spelling his name in many different ways and the family tradition, before his time, of sometimes calling themselves Shakestaff.

The years of his early adulthood are particularly problematical, and the period between the birth of his twins in 1585 and his definite establishment on the London theatre scene, are usually known as "the lost years." There have been countless theories about what he got up to in these seven years. Some say he travelled about Warwickshire, sampling the various ales on offer, doing some deer-poaching, getting caught and whipped for it. The plays show he knew the ways and language of the law, so some argue that he must have worked in a law office. But he also knew the language of soldiers and sailors, so it is possible to suppose he was a soldier in the Netherlands, fighting against Spain, or a sailor in the Mediterranean. Certainly, plays like *The Tempest* and *Twelfth Night* and several more suggest a personal knowledge of Italy and the Mediterranean. But Shakespeare was a good listener and had a retentive memory, so he may have picked all this up by listening to the talk of soldiers and sailors and lawyers. The earliest written testimony comes from John Aubrey, writing 50 years after Shakespeare's death, who says he was reputed to have been "a schoolmaster in the country." None of these surmises is impossible, and it seems probable that the young man might have tried his hand at several professions before plumping for the theatre. The only certain thing is that none of them are certain.

It is possible, even, that he visited the far north of England.

Recent research – chiefly by Professor E.A.J.Honigmann of Newcastle University, has put forward a case for the following scenario: that when he left grammar school at 16 Shakespeare, through the recommendation of one of his Stratford teachers, got a job as assistant teacher at the Lancashire home of a wealthy and well-connected Roman Catholic called Alexander Hoghton (Hoghton Tower is still there, near Preston), and that – after returning home to marry and beget his first child – he went back to Lancashire to join the company of actors in the service of Lord Strange, who was a friend of the Hoghtons.

Alexander Hoghton, who died in 1581, left in his will £2 and "play clothes and musical instruments" to one "William Shakeshafte now dwelling with me." Could this be yet another variant on our William's variable name? There is other ingenious evidence, none of it conclusive but certainly suggestive. It implies that Shakespeare may have begun his professional career in the theatre in the mid-1580's several years earlier than previously supposed, and even that he might have been a Roman Catholic in his adolescence and early manhood.

If Shakespeare got himself as far north as the Preston region, did he venture further north? The idea ties in – or may tie in – with an old tale about Muncaster Castle on the Cumbrian coast near Ravenglass. The steward of the castle in Shakespeare's time was a notable eccentric and wit called Thomas Skelton, who was also a jester or "Fool." He is said to have been a friend of Shakespeare's who certainly enjoyed the company of accomplished "fools" and wrote some wonderful parts for them in his plays. And there is a persistent tradition at Muncaster that Shakespeare went there to see his friend – no date given, no hard evidence of any kind, just an old handed-down story like those about the beds that Queen Elizabeth 1 slept in all over England.

Thomas Skelton is said to have given the word "Tomfoolery" to the English language. As with many of the fools in Shakespeare's plays, there was a dark side to his humour. He was a compulsive practical-joker. Another Muncaster tale is that he would spend many hours, in good weather, lying beneath the great tree near the castle entrance, reading. The public path ran close by and his reading was occasionally interrupted by travellers seeking the quickest route into Eskdale. If they inquired courteously, Skelton would give them clear and proper directions. But if their manner was imperious or condescending or offensive in any way, he would give equally clear directions that led straight into dangerous quicksands in the estuary.

A more up-to-date, and far less tenuous, Cumbria/ Shakespeare connection takes us back to Kendal. It was there, in September 1909, that a boy was born whose name was Geoffrey Bragg. His father was a clerk in a woolen mill. At the age of seven Geoffrey went to the grammar school, and the great event of his early life came soon afterwards. The actor-manager Sir Frank Benson arrived in town with his company of touring players, to present several Shakespeare plays.

"Never will I forget, "Geoffrey wrote many years later, "the first night in St. George's Hall, an old horseshoe-like theatre with an antiquated roller curtain with advertisements painted on it. Behind that curtain there was a new world born to me that night, a world of romance, of wonderful people who seemed like gods ... from then on until today the theatre has been real to me, and the world has been somehow make-believe. I determined then and there that I would somehow, someday, be in that real world."

He began attending a local acting class, in an upper room in Lowther Street, and got small parts in amateur productions. He left school at 16 and worked as an office boy in an engineering firm, hating it – his heart, and all his spare time, were devoted to theatre. When the Benson company returned to Kendal in 1927, he got walk-on parts. A year later he gave up his job to join a repertory company at the Royalty theatre, Morecambe.

From this moment on, he was a theatre man. He married a young actress called Laura, became an actor-manager with his own touring company, and changed his name to that of his home town, Geoffrey Kendal. "Bragg was not thought sufficiently theatrical," he explained – although in more recent times Melvyn of that ilk (whom God preserve! of Wigton) has not done too badly in the media world without bothering to change his name.

In the Second World War Geoffrey and Laura Kendal joined E.N.S.A., which stood for Entertainment National Service Association and took shows to servicemen all over the world. Soldiers used to call it, not always unfairly, "Every Night Something Awful." In 1944 they sailed out to India to join a company, commanded by Colonel Jack Hawkins, that toured the land with productions of the classics, Shakespeare especially. It was the start of another love affair for Kendal – with India. He, and Laura, adored the colour and variety and the vivid quality of life they found there, the dramatic extremes. And they loved the audiences, so eager and intelligent and responsive – "the most rewarding audiences in the world," he said.

They enjoyed India so much that after the war they formed their own company, called Shakespearana, and went out again to spend years touring all over that vast country, presenting a repertoire of classic plays (mostly Shakespeare again) in schools and village halls and city theatres. They became famous. He was known as "The Shakespeare Wallah." They had two daughters, Jennifer and Felicity, who first appeared on stage at the age of nine months as The Changeling Boy in *A Midsummer Night's Dream* and was playing Puck in the same play by the time she was nine.

In 1963 they were approached by a young team of film-makers – Ismail Merchant, James Ivory and the writer Ruth Jhabvala – who wanted to make a film about their work. Geoffrey disliked all the fuss and time-wasting and endless re-takes of filming, and suspected they were presenting him as a "ham" actor rather than a serious evangelist for Shakespeare, but the film, also called "The Shakespeare Wallah," came out in 1964 and was a great success.

Another man of Cumbrian origin, who travelled far afield and became a great Shakespearian but who never achieved Kendal's fame, was Joseph Crosby. He was born in the village of Kirkby Thore on the River Eden in what was then Westmorland, in July 1821. His family had been yeoman farmers in that region for centuries, and are still there. Joseph was born in Powis House which is farmed today by John David Crosby, not a direct descendant of Joseph but of the ninth generation of Crosby's to farm there.

Joseph was clearly not cut out for the farming life. At Appleby School his interest was in languages and reading, especially Shakespeare. He went on to Queens College, Oxford, to study the ancient languages, and in 1834 emigrated to the

United States to work with an uncle in a grocery business in Zanesville, Ohio.

He was not cut out for the grocery business either, but he stuck at it and consoled himself by devoting all his spare cash and leisure time to collecting books by and about Shakespeare and writing long, learned letters to another fanatic, a Philadelphia lawyer called Joseph Parker Norris. The provincial Mid-West of the United States, in the years before and during the Civil War, cannot have been an encouraging environment for such a man as Crosby, but his enthusiasm never waned. He even founded a Zanesville Shakespeare Reading Club, and presided over its meetings for many years. He amassed a great collection of books that included 175 complete Shakespeare editions, dating between 1709 and 1881. When the grocery business went to the wall in the depression of the 1880's, all the books had to be sold. It must have been heartbreaking for Crosby. Perhaps he was cheered a little by being described in the auctioneer's catalogue as one of only three Americans who could claim to be learned Shakespearians "in an eminent sense."

His letters to Norris were published in the United States in 1986 and make impressive reading for anyone interested in Shakespeare, for Crosby was not only encyclopaedic in his knowledge of the great man's works and meticulous in his scholarship, he also showed a thoughtful and sensible approach and a breadth of sympathy and appreciation that do not always go with great scholarship.

In one letter he said: "One touch of Shakespeare makes the whole world kin."

The Wordsworths, William and his sister Dorothy, did not read widely but they read deeply. Their library was small – a handful of classics, particularly Chaucer and Milton and

Shakespeare. Dorothy's Grasmere *Journal* repeatedly mentions plays of Shakespeare they are reading. Shakespeare, as many have remarked, was universal, for all moods and for all time, the ultimate and unrivalled portrayer of the human condition. It is a great shame he never walked the Lakeland fells. If he had, I suspect, he would certainly have described the landscape, somewhere in the plays, in language of incomparable power and accuracy. What he did do, and it seems very remarkable to me, two centuries before Wordsworth came along, was to proclaim the basic Wordsworth message, in words that Wordsworth himself never surpassed. At the beginning of the second act of *As You Like It,* the Duke, banished from his palace and living rough in the Forest of Arden, seeks to reassure his attendant lords with these words:

> *"... and this our life, exempt from public haunt,*
> *Finds tongues in trees, books in the running brooks,*
> *Sermons in stone, and good in everything."*

You cannot get more Wordsworthian than that.

Skiddaw's Glory

Our hero this time is not a literary luminary, not a human being at all, but a much more imposing and venerable Lake District figure, the mountain called Skiddaw. Until 200 years or so ago it was generally believed that Skiddaw's summit was the highest point of land in England. In 1755 Dr. John Dalton wrote a *descriptive poem* which proclaimed:

> *Supreme of mountains, Skiddaw, hail!*
> *To whom all Britain sinks a vale!...*

In fact as everyone now knows, Skiddaw is only the fourth highest mountain in the Lake District. It has, however, another, and this time irrefutable, claim to fame – the fact that its stony summit has been visited by an impressive list of distinguished people. Most of them were writers, and virtually all of them left some account of their climbs.

One of the earliest of them – he ascended Skiddaw on a Sunday in September 1799 – who was not a writer but became the figurehead and political leader of England's first and still one of its most effective, pressure groups. This was William Wilberforce, campaigner for the abolition of the infamous slave trade. In 1799, though, he was a student at Cambridge, spending a month of the long summer vacation in the part of England he had come to love best.

He kept a diary of the Lakeland trip, and for that day, September 12th, he noted: "After church took a snack and went up Skiddaw. When we had got about half way to the top, the day grew thick and was never fine afterwards throughout; it was quite clear almost all round except into Borrodale etc. by little slips at a Time. The Sun shone very bright upon the Sea, upon which six or seven ships were seen quite plain with the naked eye. The view into Northumberland and Scotland is very extensive. The Isle of Man is very visible … you see a Hill which is said by the Guide to be near Newcastle…"

The guide, is must be said, was a Keswick man called Thomas Hutton, notorious for giving information to his clients that was fascinating and impressive but also completely inaccurate. Sometimes he convinced them they were looking at the North Sea.

Although it was summer, it was cold on the summit, as it usually is on Skiddaw; "The Air is very cold at the top," he noted, "and the wind almost always very high. Upon it are two Heaps of Stones, upon which people who generally write their names… One may go up on Horseback the greater Part of the Way."

The 18th century mountaineers always hired a guide, and most of them hired horses too, to carry them and their provisions up.

Fifteen years after Wilberforce's visit, a retired army captain called Joseph Budworth, who had lost an arm at the siege of Gibralter, spent a fortnight touring the Lake District, eating prodigious meals, appreciating the local girls, and hiring shepherds to lead him to the fell tops. Budworth used his own legs, not horses, and found the mountain air and adventure invigorating. He made the long slog up Skiddaw from Keswick, and was rewarded with an all-round, sunset view of remarkable clarity.

"When we reach the top," he wrote, "we open the crown of Ingleborough, and the range of hills to the champaign part of Northumberland; we have the Cheviot hills, and the great chain to the point of Mull in Galloway," He also claimed they could make out the Irish Sea beyond Whitehaven and "upwards of 20 vessels under sail," the whole of the Isle of Man, and even the coast of Northern Ireland.

It was an east wind, which explains the clearness of the views.

"We were at the farthest heap of stones, covered from the East wind when I wrote the above; the air was thin and cool, but when we took our departure, we were obliged to run over the hard surface as quick as we could, and before we were under cover from the wind, drops (not poetical) ran down our cheeks, and saving your presence, uninvited, from my nose; my fingers were almost benumbed; but when we came under cover from the wind, we took time to breathe, and found the evening soft and fine."

Two years after Budworth, Skiddaw had a very different visitor. This was Ann Radcliffe, a successful novelist in the "Gothic horror" style that was highly popular at the time, melodramatic tales of cruelty and terror and startling incident, usually set in ruined monasteries and wilderness landscapes. Her best-known book *The Mysteries of Udolpho* was published in 1794, and it was in that year that she rode to the top of Skiddaw on a horse. Her account of the adventure displays all the inventive powers that she put into her novels. Like Budworth, she had a local guide and they followed the main tourist path from Keswick: "About a mile from the summit, the way was indeed dreadfully sublime, lying, for nearly half a mile, along the edge of the precipice, that passed with a swift descent, for probably near a mile, into a glen within the heart of Skiddaw... The hill rose so closely above the precipice, as scarcely to allow a ledge wide enough for a single horse. We followed the guide in silence, and till we regained the more open wild, had no leisure for exclamation."

People usually exaggerate their adventures a little when writing them up afterwards, but this is ridiculous. Nowadays, thousands of people walk up this path each year, ranging from six-year-olds to octogenarians, and not one of them sees the "precipices" that Mrs. Radcliffe saw on all sides. Terror, like beauty, must be in the eyes of the beholder, and it is certainly a fact that many 18th century tourists found "horrifying chasms" and "impending cliffs" at every turn of the path. No doubt, they were encouraged in these fears by their shepherd/guides who wanted them to feel sure they were getting their money's-worth of security and *frisson* .

Like Budworth, Mrs. Radcliffe was rewarded with wonderful, long-distance views to the Irish Sea and across the Solway Firth and eastwards to "what we were told were the Cheviot hills." It was cold on top, but they soon descended into summer warmth to reach Keswick at 4 p.m., "after five hours passed in this excursion, in which the care of our guide greatly lessened the notion of danger."

Four years later the mountain was ascended by an even more unlikely person, the Anglican clergyman Sydney Smith. He was the opposite of Mrs. Radcliffe in almost every way – cool, rational, witty, an unashamed lover of city life and dinner parties, not at all inclined to go into fashionable raptures about wild landscapes. He defined the country as "a kind of healthy grave," and also said: "In the country I always fear that creation will expire before tea-time."

Even so, passing through the Lake District in the early summer of 1798, he arranged an expedition up Skiddaw for himself and the boy he was escorting.

161

"Off we set, Michael, the guide and myself, at one in the morning. I, who find it rather difficult to stick upon my horse on the plainest roads, did not find that facility increased by the darkness of the morning or the precipitous paths we had to ascend. I made no manner of doubt but that I should roll down into the town of Keswick the next morning and be picked up by the town beadle dead in the gutter."

It is not clear why they made such an early start, but, sustained by brandy, they gained the summit, found it cold and gusty and wreathed in cloud, so they had more brandy and some biscuits and waited for the views to emerge at sunrise. They were back in Keswick for a "monstrous breakfast."

Another confirmed big-city man Charles Lamb of London, all-round literary man and essayist and lifelong friend of Samuel Taylor Coleridge, was in Keswick in August 1802. He and his sister Mary were guests of the Coleridges at Greta Hall. They took the opportunity of tackling the local mountain.

"Mary was excessively tired," Lamb said in a letter, "when she got about half-way up Skiddaw, but we came to a cold rill, and with the reinforcement of a draught of cold water she surmounted it most manfully. Oh, its fine black head, and the bleak air atop of it, with a prospect of mountains all about, and about, making you giddy; and then Scotland afar off, and the border counties so famous in song and ballad! It was a day that will stand out, like a mountain, I am sure, in my life."

Lamb wrote this on his return to London. He was beginning to consider the rival claims of London and the Lake District.

"I find I shall conform in time to that state of life to which it has pleased God to call me. Besides, after all, Fleet Street and the Strand are better places to live in for good and all than among

Skiddaw. Still, I turn back to those great places where I wandered about, participating in their greatness. After all, I could not *live* in Skiddaw. I could spend a year-two, three years among them but I must have a prospect of seeing Fleet Street at the end of that time, or I should mope and pine away, I know. Still, Skiddaw is a fine creature."

Coleridge had none of his friend's doubts on this matter. At this time of his life Coleridge saw the city as a kind of prison, and believed that the closer a man lived with nature the better it would be for his character and soul. He loved the wilderness and wild weather, and responded to them with whole-hearted passion. He was the first person to go up into the fells for nothing more than the fun and excitement of it, the first genuine fell walker. He would go out, in rain or winds or darkness, getting off the beaten paths to explore the steep places and the ridges, usually on his own: ..."for I must be alone," he wrote, "if either my imagination or heart are to be excited or enriched."

He went to the top of Skiddaw in 1800, only a few weeks after his family had moved into Greta Hall. In a letter to a friend he said: "I was standing on the very top of Skiddaw, by a little shed of slate-stones on which I had scribbled with a bit of slate my name among the other names – a lean expressive-faced man came up the hill, stood beside me a little while, then running over the names, exclaimed 'Coleridge: I lay my life that is the poet Coleridge.'"

The other Lake Poets – William Wordsworth and Robert Southey – knew Skiddaw summit too. They were there together, with members of their families, on the night of August 21st, 1815, for a great bonfire to celebrate the final victory over Napoleon at Waterloo. Southey described it brilliantly in a letter.

"The weather served for our bonfire, and never, I believe,

was such an assemblage upon such a spot. To my utter astonishment, Lord Sunderlin rode up, and Lady S. joined the walking party. Wordsworth, with his wife, sister and eldest boy, came over on purpose. James Boswell (son of the biographer of Dr. Johnson) arrived that morning at the Sunderlins. Edith, the Senora, Edith May and Herbert were my convoy, with our three maidservants, some of our neighbours, some adventurous Lakers, and Messers Rag, Tag and Bobtail made up the rest of the assembly. We roasted beef, and boiled plum puddings there; sung 'God save the King' round the most furious body of flaming tar-barrels that I ever saw; drank a large wooden bowl of punch; fired canon at every health with three times three, and rolled large blazing balls of tow and turpentine down the steep side of the mountain. The effect was beyond imagination. We formed a huge circle round the most intense light and behind us was an immeasurable arch of the most intense darkness, for our bonfire fairly put out the moon."

There have been midnight bonfires on top of Skiddaw since – mostly organized by Canon Rawnsley for national celebrations like Queen Victoria's Diamond Jubilee – but there has probably been nothing like that Waterloo party in 1815, and it seems certain that the National Park authorities would not allow such riotous goings-on nowadays.

The catalogue continues. John Keats climbed Skiddaw in 1818, drinking rum to keep warm and said: "I felt as if I were going to a Tournament." John Ruskin, at the age of 12 went up with a large holiday party, with guide and ponies, and described the adventure in a long doggerel poem called *Iteriad.*

In this century the novelist Hugh Walpole was taken up by George Abraham, the Keswick climber/photographer, and was so impressed by the setting of Skiddaw House – "one of the loneliest dwelling-places in all the British Isles – that he made it the scene of one of his great dramatic incidents in *The Herries Chronicles,* a fatal family duel followed by a suicide. A later novelist, Melvyn Bragg, lives just north of Skiddaw in the holidays and often explores the region. And Ken Russell, the aging Enfant Terrible of the British film business, fell in love with the Lake District at first sight (though only temporarily) when he threw open the bedroom curtains in the Lodore Swiss Hotel's attic: "My heart pounded, my blood raced, I caught my breath, my eyes widened, my hair stood on end, an unseen orchestra played a tremendous chord. Only clichés can describe what no one has ever been able to portray – a vision of God … From my window in the turret, Skiddaw dominated the entire landscape. Before me stretched three miles of Derwentwater, its shores reaching to Keswick and dominating Keswick like a great pterodactyl with a wingspan of seven miles was Skiddaw, and if the Christian God is three in one, then Skiddaw, the pagan god is nine in one – Latrigg, Dodd, Longside, Jenkin Hill, Ullock Pike, Lonscale Fell, Carl Side and Little Man – these eight lesser hills forming part of one almighty godhead, SKIDDAW."

Even Skiddaw, old in story, had never heard such praise before. Russell had travelled north to make a film for television, but he soon had a home in Borrowdale and made several films there in the 1980's. He said the Lake District replaced Roman Catholicism as his spiritual sustenance, and he probably meant it at the time, though he has moved on subsequently. He also said that Skiddaw and the Newlands Fells, viewed from Borrowdale, always reminded him of naked, prostrate women. But then almost everything – almost anything – seems to remind Ken Russell of naked prostrate women.

Arthur Ransome

Arthur Ransome is now remembered chiefly as the writer of the series of children's stories that started with Swallows and Amazons in 1930 and went on appearing, one a year, into the early 1940's. They have been continuously in print ever since, more than four and a half million copies have been sold, and have generated films and television serials. But there is much more to Ransome than that. He was a successful journalist and foreign correspondent, an excellent translator from the Russian, a serious and thoughtful writer on literary subjects, a marvellous writer about fishing and small boat sailing, and the sometime adviser

Above: Arthur Ransome's cottage at Low Ludderburn

Arthur Ransome at leisure

and friend of national leaders like Lloyd George and Ramsay MacDonald, Lenin and Trotsky. He was also a remarkably complex and individual personality, full of unexpected quirks and apparent contradictions.

By nature he was an extrovert, a man of vigour and courage, enjoying adventure. But physically he was frail, short-sighted from the first and the life-long victim of ulcers and other disorders of the gut. He had an independent spirit but he was also a great worrier, the prey of self-doubts and perplexities. Journalism took him across the world and into the company of many grand and powerful people, yet his approach to life remained unworldly, naïve almost. He was a natural democrat, preferring the company and conversation of gypsies and charcoal-burners and fishermen. He was affectionate and convivial and could be highly entertaining, but he could also, when the mood took him, be extremely grumpy and difficult. Although the mind was clear and strong and incisive, in appearance he was the opposite – usually in scruffy old tweeds and baggy trousers, with spectacles and a big bushy, rather ragged moustache, generally puffing away on his pipe. He travelled widely and often moved home, but from childhood onwards his heart was fixed on one part of the world only, the area of lakes and fells around the shores of Coniston and Windermere. One of the strengths of Swallows and Amazons and the stories that

Arthur Ransome at work

followed arises from his deep knowledge of, and love of the Lake District.

The Lake District was one of his father's great gifts to the young Arthur. The family holidayed in the Coniston region every summer and the boy spent long, happy days sailing, fishing and exploring. Fishing was the other gift from his father. But apart from this, he had little cause to be grateful to his parents. They were undemonstrative and devoid of sympathy and understanding.

It was a long time before anyone realized that the trouble with the boy was not stupidity but acute shortsightedness. He was sent away to prep school and then public school, where he was no good at games and an easy target for the bullies. His father, Professor of History at Leeds University, was ambitious for his son, and overbearing, endlessly chivvying him to work harder and do better in the exams. It was not until he was at Leeds University himself, studying science, that Arthur summoned up the courage to break away. He was already a keen reader and had been trying his hand at the writing of stories, and now he escaped to London and got a job as office boy in a publishing house. Soon he was selling stories and articles to the magazines, and by the age of 20 he was a whole-hearted "Bohemian," with just enough income to live in Soho, eating sparingly but drinking each evening with artists and writers, talking endlessly and greatly enjoying himself. The hack-journalist Edward Thomas, later to be a fine poet, was one of the group.

Among Ransome's favourite books was the saga of Viking life in ancient Cumbria, Thorstein of the Mere, and it was in the summer of 1903, on holiday in the Coniston area, that Ransome met the author of that book, W.G. Collingwood. Collingwood asked the young man to call on him at Lanehead on the north-eastern shores of Coniston Water. He did so and was swept into a world that suited him exactly, a big and loving and lively family, careless of convention but cheerfully serious about art and work and play. He was captivated. In his autobiography, written half a century later, Ransome said of the Collingwoods: "The whole of the rest of my life has been happier because of them." They all worked hard in the morning – painting, writing, reading – then spent the afternoons on or around the lake. The Collingwoods' boat was called Swallow. After this he returned to the Coniston region each summer, sometimes bringing literary friends from London. He published a few books, including one about the Bohemian life of Soho, another about the American writer Edgar Allan Poe.

For a while he was in love with one of the Collingwood daughters, but though the whole family was very fond of him, the love was not reciprocated and he turned instead, and disastrously, to a good-looking, but emotionally unstable woman called Ivy Walker. They married in 1909. At his publisher's suggestion, Arthur wrote a book about Oscar Wilde, a bold undertaking since nothing had been written about the great wit and playwright since his conviction, 15 years before, for homosexual activities. He did the writing well and carefully but this did not prevent Lord Alfred Douglas, the chief cause of Wilde's downfall from suing for libel when the book came out. It was a nightmare time for Arthur Ransome. His wife loved all the publicity and acrimony and angst, but he hated it. The trial lasted four days and the verdict was in Ransome's favour but he was simply glad the ordeal was over. Soon after he set off for Russia, to get away from his wife and to learn the Russian language with a view to translating fairy tales into English.

He liked Russia and its people. When the First World War began and Russia came in on our side, he was hired by the Daily News to be their correspondent on the Russian front. It was a dangerous time but he was a man of natural courage and calm. It grew even more dangerous when Russia collapsed in 1917, pulled out of the war and took to violent revolution. Ransome, in St. Petersburg was in the thick of it, played chess with Lenin (who was not much good, apparently) and with Litvinov (who was better), and fell in love with Trotsky's personal secretary, Evgenia. It was a thrilling time and Ransome enjoyed it, but he was often desperately homesick, not for London and his family but for the Lake District. He kept two pictures of the fells on the desk where he worked and a sprig of heather from Peel Island on Coniston Water. In a letter home he said: "I want to see the hills. I think of them all the time."

He finally decided to get out of Russia and take Evgenia with him, and they walked through the lines of the Red Army and across no-man's land and then through the lines of the White Russian forces, Ransome smoking his pipe all the while to indicate his innocent neutrality. They got to Estonia and lived there for a few years. He was now writing for the Manchester Guardian and such spare time as he got they spent sailing small boats on the Baltic.

In the mid – 1920's they came to England and made immediately for the southern Lake District. He was divorced by this time so free to marry Evgenia. On a remote hillside less than a mile from the eastern shores of Windermere they found an old sturdily-built but very run-down cottage called Low Ludderburn.

It had a barn and a lovely, abundant garden and a superb view across the Winster Valley. It was primitive – no running water, no electricity, full of low beams on which they both banged their heads repeatedly – but they were a tough and capable couple and saw at once as he wrote to his mother, that it was capable of being pulled about and turned into an almost perfect place, bit by bit. They got it for £550 freehold and set about it. The house still stands, quite smart now and graced with the basic mod. cons., but looking from the outside very much as it must have done in 1925 when the Ransomes moved in.

He was comfortably established now both as an author and as a journalist. Books about the Russian Revolution and small boat-sailing on the Baltic had been well-received. The Manchester Guardian was sending him all over – to Egypt, to China – as a special correspondent, and he was writing a weekly column for them about fishing. At last, it seemed, he could be financially secure and settled. But there was a sort of divine discontent about Ransome, a sense of unfulfilment, the feeling that he really ought to be doing a different sort of writing altogether.

In 1928 one of the Collingwood daughters Dora, who had married an Amernian doctor, Ernest Altounyan, paid a long summer visit to Coniston with their five children. Their father, with some help from Ransome, bought them a couple of sailing dinghies and the children, with a lot of help from Ransome, learned to sail and fish, camp and explore the lake and its islands.

Through their excitement, Ransome recaptured his own childhood delights. And through them, he was now to find his true métier as a writer.

He was firm with the children but got on well with them and in the evening would entertain them with stories and old songs, especially sea shanties, that he would play on the penny whistle he always carried. He was sad and rather lost when the Altounyans returned to their home in Aleppo, and felt restless throughout the winter that followed. Next spring, he got one of the dinghies out, the one that had been called Swallow in honour of the old Collingwood boat, and started to sail it alone. The idea for a children's adventure story began to grow in his mind. He started to write it down in his little cluttered study at Low Ludderburn, and the narrative flowed.

He wrote the story, which became Swallows and Amazons, in the face of considerable obstacles. His health was bad. His wife was discouraging, insisting that he should get on with his journalism and make them some money. The Manchester Guardian was putting great pressure on him to take a full-time job with them. He enjoyed writing the book but was not at all sure the result would be worthwhile. But he persisted, and in April 1930 sent the completed manuscript to Jonathan Cape, the publishers. It came out in July and was a success. So much so that in the next 17 years he wrote eleven sequel stories about the same children and their sailing adventures.

In a note written in 1958, about the writing of Swallows and Amazons Ransome said that the initial impetus had come from his memories of childhood holidays by Coniston Water: "We adored the place. Coming to it we used to run down to the lake, dip our hands in and wish, as if we had just seen the new moon. Going away from it we were half drowned in tears. While away from it, as children and as grown ups, we dreamt about it. No matter where I was, wandering about the world, I used at night to look for the North Star and, in my mind's eye, could see the beloved skyline of great hills beneath it. Swallows and Amazons grew out of those old memories. I could not help writing it. It almost wrote itself."

The books are still read and loved by many children, and re-read from time to time by many adults who loved them when they were young. Some folk complain that the stories seem dated now, too middle class and well-conducted. No modern children, they say, would behave so politely and sensibly and be so obedient to their parents as Ransome's children are. It may well, sadly, be so. The behaviour of English children has changed greatly in 60 years and so, too, has the Lake District. But the stories are still exciting.

For one thing, Ransome was writing about things he knew well – the land and the water of Coniston and Windermere, the special skills required for sailing and fishing and camping, the charcoal burners and farmers of the fell country. For another, he was a careful and accomplished craftsman with words. His style is simple and unpretentious, realistic and effective. The words and the sentences are short. There is little description, mostly just the plain facts, what the children did and saw and said and imagined. The adventures they have are perfectly possible ones. No great emotional depths are plumbed, but the narrative is always clear and pacy. In many ways Ransome was very child-like himself and he was always aware of the rich imaginative life that children lead. This is one of the strengths of the books. All young children feel that there is an enormous gulf between them and the grown-ups, and the children in these stories invariably think of themselves as pirates, explorers and adventurers, and regard adults as "natives," sometimes friendly and sometimes hostile but always quite different.

Ransome once said: "You write not for children but for yourself, and if, by good fortune, children enjoy what you enjoy, why then you are a writer of children's books...... No special credit to you, but simply thumping good luck."

His good luck came to him in mid-life; he was 48 when he wrote Swallows and Amazons, and its sequel kept him occupied until he was past 60. His financial problems were solved, his fame assured. Over the years he was awarded an honary Doctorate of letters at Leeds University, a C.B.E., and the Library Associations's Carnegie Medal. He went on fishing and sailing and chatting to ordinary, working people, but ill health, his and his wife's, was an increasing problem. They moved house often. When they went from the Lake District to live for a while in Suffolk, a removal firm in Kendal helped with the move. Ransome offered the driver a bed for the night before he set off on the long drive home and was delighted by the reply "Nay, Mr Ransome. I want to get back to England."Before the end, Ransome got back to his own favourite part of England. He died in 1967 and lies buried in the churchyard in the Rusland Valley.

Recent years have seen a remarkable upsurge of interest in Arthur Ransome, the man and his life and his work. It began, I suppose, on the centenary of his birth, in 1984, when his old publishers, Cape, published, Hugh Brogan's admirable biography. There have been other good books about him since. And in 1990, the Arthur Ransome society was formed to keep interest in him alive and to spread the word, especially to children. At the Abbot Hall Museum of Lakeland Life and Industry in Kendal, the society has lovingly recreated the room at Low Ludderburn where Ransome sat and wrote Swallows and

Amazons, with his desk and typewriter, his books and pictures (those he drew to illustrate his stories), his chess set and some of the pipes that he puffed continuously while the adventures unfolded on the white paper before him.

Harriet Martineau: The Knoll

Harriet Martineau was already a highly successful writer and in her mid-40's when she built her home in Ambleside. The house is still there, still a private dwelling. She called it The Knoll, because it stands on a steep rocky mound on the northern outskirts of the town, commanding a westwards view across the fields to the river Rothay and the friendly slopes of Loughrigg Fell beyond. From the outside, the house looks exactly as it must have done when it was first built in the winter of 1845. Like its creator, it is sturdy and practical and without pretension. The

Above: The Knoll with Harriet Martineau's sundial in the foreground

house itself and the terrace wall in the garden are made of dark grey Westmorland stone. They look as if they will last for ever.

Not many people nowadays remember Harriet Martineau or read her books but she was, in her day, a famous and formidable woman. She was independent-minded. She could express herself with clarity and force. She felt very strongly about the evils of English life, especially the callous treatment of the poor, and dedicated herself to reform. In an age of wide-spread religious

Harriet Martineau

bigotry and hypocrisy and intolerance, these qualities were bound to make her many enemies, but she was never for one moment deterred or distracted from her life's work.

At first sight, there would seem to be absolutely nothing in common between Harriet Martineau and Beatrix Potter except the fact that they both made a lot of money from writing. In the shape of their two lives, however, there is a strong parallel. Both of them were condemned, until middle age, to frustration and unhappiness. "My life," Harriet wrote, "has had no Spring." Each of them then broke away from the past and came to live in the Lake District. Each lived happily ever after, though in very different ways. Years later, writing her *Autobiography* and reflecting on the transformation of her life, Harriet said: "During this last sunny period I have felt for the first time, a keen and unvarying relish for life."

She grew up in Norwich in the early years of the last century. It was a large family, piously Unitarian and reasonably well-off. But Harriet, from the start, was made miserable. She was a sickly child, sensitive and timid, easily hurt and frightened. She had five elder brothers and sisters who liked to upset and humiliate her. Her mother, strict and humourless, denied her any sign of affection. She was also a very plain little girl, awkward in movement, often in tears, occasionally exploding into rage at the unfairness of the world. In addition to all this, she was hard of hearing. For a long time, as often happens, her deafness was taken as a sign of perversity or stupidity or both.

But Harriet was very far from being stupid. She had a clear, logical and retentive mind. She read, and thought about what she read, and developed the habit of hard study. About the age of 20 she found she could write both fluently and well. At first, her work was devotional, propagating the Unitarian cause. Then she widened her range and took to writing stories that always had a serious moral purpose, usually concerned with the lives of poor people in the new manufacturing towns and cities of England. To her surprise, they proved immensely popular. It is not the sort of stuff that makes best-seller material in the latter part of the 20th century, but Victorian readers were more sentimental than we are and more serious-minded about social issues. When Harriet went to London in 1831 she was acclaimed and lionized in a way that we reserve for pop singers and sports stars.

Success did not corrupt her. She went on working hard – researching carefully into the problems of the poor, the effects of taxation and the Poor Laws, the right of working people to form trade unions, then creating stories to illustrate the themes. She went to the United States and risked lynching in the South by speaking out against the slave system. She went to the coronation of the Queen in 1837 and condemned the service as idolatrous, confusing the worship of God with the worship of the monarch. She met everyone in London who mattered and though she offended some, she made friends with many. But she had no presumptuous illusions about herself. Speaking about her writing, she said: "I have not done it for amusement, or for money, or for fame, or for any other reason but because I could not help it... Things were pressing to be said, and there was more or less evidence that I was the person to say them." She also said: "Of posthumous fame I have not the slightest expectation or desire. To be useful in my day and generation is enough for me."

Then she fell seriously ill. For more than five years, from 1839, she thought she was a dying woman. It was during this period, oddly enough, that she lost her Christian faith and became what would now be called an agnostic, though the word had not been coined at that time. Then, in desperation, conventional medicine having apparently failed, she turned to the new quack science of mesmerism. Within a few months she was well again, to remain convinced for the rest of her life that suggestion under hypnosis had a powerful healing role to play.

To complete her recovery, she took a month's holiday at Waterhead, Windermere. She loved the Lake District landscape and determined to return soon and find a way of leading a more open-air life. What she needed, she said, was a house of her own among "poor improvable neighbours, with young servants whom I might train and attach to myself; with pure air, a garden, leisure, solitude at command, and freedom to work in peace and quietness." It is a tribute to the clarity of her vision, and the forcefulness of her character, that that is exactly what she created.

She bought a patch of land on the northern edge of Ambleside. She organized and oversaw the building of The

Knoll, then designed and planted her garden. Her neighbour, William Wordsworth, now 75 years old, came and planted two pine trees for her, under the terrace wall. He told her she had taken the wisest step of her life. She thought he would go on to expound the blessings of rural solitude, the uplifting influences of Nature, and was a little shocked when he added: "It is the wisest step of your life, for the value of the property will be doubled in ten years."

The old poet also advised her that she would find visitors a great expense. "When you have a visitor," he said, "you must do as we did, you must say: if you like to have a cup of tea with us you are very welcome, but if you want any meat, you must pay for your board." She managed, with difficulty, to get away without promising to do that.

Harriet was anxious to avoid getting too involved in local society – she dreaded the gossip and feuding she knew it would involve – but she had good friends in the area and many of her old friends came to visit and stay. There was a new friend, too, the novelist Charlotte Bronte. Miss Bronte spent more than a week at The Knoll in December 1850 and was very impressed by the character of her hostess: "She is not a person to be judged by her writings alone, but rather by her own deeds and life, than which nothing can be more exemplary or nobler. She seems to me the benefactress of Ambleside, yet takes no sort of credit to herself for her active and indefatigable philanthropy."

Miss Martineau, running her household, entertaining her guests, researching and writing more books and countless articles, still found energy and time to tackle the problems of Ambleside head on. In a letter she wrote in June 1850 (now in the Armitt Library, Ambleside), she outlined the problem in her usual forceful style: "We are blessed with a site for a town as perfect as Nature could give us. It is made up of slopes, rocks and running streams, yet the town is abominable in all Sanitary respects. The people live in stinking holes, scrofula and consumption abound, whole families are huddled together in single rooms. The consequence of the profligacy of the place is awful. There is scarcely a girl who is not a mother before she is a wife, and the young men, finding their homes disgusting, go to the public house. Yet everyone earns good wages. We have no pauperism, except through sottishness. The people are willing and able to pay good rents, but no dwellings for labourers are built while large houses are rising in all directions with the worst set of landed proprietors."

She did more than just write about it. She lectured local folk on the evils of drink. She lectured the local builders on the need for underground sewers. She designed a model cottage that could be built for £130. She built a row of workers' cottages and created a building society, sometimes claimed to be the world's first, to enable the tenants to buy their homes as they paid rents. On her own fields she created a two-acre farm. She hired an experienced labourer, built a cottage for him, and then worked with him to make the tiny experimental farm keep the household supplied with milk and butter and cheese, fresh eggs and fresh vegetables, hams and bacon. It was a success. There was produce to spare, to sell. She wrote a booklet about it, *My Farm of Two Acres,* full of factual information and sensible advice, to encourage others to follow her example.

In the midst of all this, she also found time to make a characteristically thorough exploration of the whole Lake District. Everywhere she went, she asked questions and made notes. Every aspect of Lakeland life fascinated her. But she had no time for the sentimental illusions that Wordsworth's poems had done so much to propagate, the idea that the farmers and dalesmen were all noble and natural, independent-spirited and hard-working. In Harriet's unblinkered eyes, far too many of them were stupid and superstitious and given to over-hearty drinking. As a result, the economy was declining, the region's produce was growing more and more incapable of meeting competition. The bright young people were leaving the area.

Her solution, expounded in her *Description of the English Lakes,* was typically tough-minded. The arrival of the railways would solve the problem by bringing in fresh blood and enterprise: "Having reached this pass, it is clearly best that it should go on till the primitive population, having lost its safety of isolation and independence, and kept its ignorance and grossness, shall have given place to a new set of inhabitants, better skilled in agriculture, and in every way more up to the times. It is mournful enough to meet everywhere the remnants of the old families in a reduced and discouraged condition: but if they can no longer fill the valleys with grain, and cover the hill-sides with flocks, it is right that those who can should enter upon their lands, and that knowledge, industry and temperance should find their fair field and due reward."

Harriet Martineau made her home in Ambleside for more than 30 years and she died in her first-floor bedroom at The Knoll in June 1877. She never lost the drive to do all she could to help others, especially those who most needed help. The unpopularity of her many opinions, and the ever-vigorous way in which she expressed them, made her strongly disliked in some quarters. But there were many more who admired her for her courage and compassion and for her practical intelligence. Perhaps the best tribute to her, when she died, was paid by another formidable woman of that age, Florence Nightingale. "She was," she said, "a noble woman."

Thomas Clarkson

One of the noblest moments in British history occurred in early 1807 when trading in negro slaves – from West Africa to the plantations of the Caribbean and the United States – was abolished. It was a great and hard-fought victory for the world's first pressure group in the modern manner. One of the leaders of the abolitionist movement, William Wilberforce, is widely known and acclaimed. But there was another hero of the story, every bit as dedicated and influential as Wilberforce though in an entirely different way. His name, Thomas Clarkson, is now known to few. Neither of them was Cumbrian but, by coincidence, both of

Above: Thomas Clarkson's house at Eusemere

Thomas Clarkson

them loved the landscape of the Lake District and lived there at one time or another.

Wilberforce, born in Hull was a student at Cambridge when he paid his first visit to the Lakes. He enjoyed the trip so much that he returned with some undergraduate friends for the last of his long vacations. They spent the whole of September 1779 touring the district, on horseback and on foot, admiring waterfalls and echo-effects and the wild "prospects" in the correct fashion of pioneer "picturesque" tourists. They had characteristic weather – it seems to have rained every other day – but managed to make many adventurous excursions, always attended by a local guide. They walked over Stake Pass to Langdale and over Newlands Pass to Buttermere. They climbed Castle Crag and Skiddaw.

Wilberforce kept a diary and made a note of his observations from the summit of Skiddaw: "The sun shone very bright upon the Sea, upon which six or seven Ships were seen quite plain with the naked eye. The view into Northumberland and Scotland is very extensive... You see a Hill which is said by the Guide to be near Newcastle." Their guide was a Keswick man, Thomas Hutton, notorious for giving his clients wonderful but completely misleading information.

The year after this trip Wilberforce took a seven-year lease on Rayrigg Hall, on the eastern shores of Windermere, staying there whenever he could. He spoke of the Lake District as "this Region of Wonders" and "this earthly Paradise," and was lavish with the fashionable adjectives, "sublime" and "majestic." It made the rest of England, he said, seem insipid to him, over-tamed by man. In one letter he said that as a young man he had always felt in greater danger of falling in love when he was in wild, spectacular, romantic country. For all the intense busyness of his later years – as an MP for Yorkshire and political figurehead of the abolitionist cause – he visited the district when he could and thought about it when he could not.

Thomas Clarkson grew up in Cambridgeshire, and arrived at the university as Wilberforce left it. Clarkson was a serious young man. He studied and in his final year won a university prize for an essay in Latin on the subject: Is it right to make men slaves against their will?

He researched hard and produced a powerful condemnation of the idea of slavery, but it was an intellectual exercise for him rather than a matter of conviction. On his way home from college following this success, he found himself thinking obsessively about the issue.

He later recalled: "I stopped my horse occasionally and dismounted and walked. I frequently tried to persuade myself in these intervals that the contents of my essay could not be true. I sat down disconsolate on the turf by the roadside and held my horse. Here a thought came into my mind – that if the contents of the essay were true, it was time some person should see these calamities to their end. Agitated in this manner, I reached home."

It did not take him long to make up his mind. He had intended to become an Anglican clergyman, but now he determined to dedicate himself to one cause, the destruction of the slave trade. He translated his essay into English and had it published. Very soon he found others, most of them Quakers, whose detestation of the slave trade was as strong as his. In May 1787 a committee was formed to campaign for its abolition.

Clarkson's first great contribution to the cause was to go and see Wilberforce to persuade him to join their campaign.

The two men were dissimilar in many ways. Clarkson was earnest and industrious, fearless and tireless, but almost entirely devoid of charm and humour and political guile. Wilberforce, on the other hand, was already making his mark as an MP, eloquent and intelligent, rich and amiable, and very well-connected. One of his closest associates was the young William Pitt, son of a great Prime Minister and soon to become Prime Minister himself at the age of 24.

In a way Clarkson was lucky in the timing of his approach, though there was no calculation in it. After Cambridge, Wilberforce had become a man-about-town, fond of dinner parties and late nights, dancing and gambling. Suddenly when he was 25, he underwent a religious conversion, repented his previous wicked ways, and determined to make amends by devoting himself to good works. He joined "the Clapham Sect," a group of evangelical Christians who abhorred the cynical laxness of the times in which they lived and were prepared to work together to cleanse society of its abuses.

So Wilberforce was ripe for persuasion when Clarkson called on him in 1787, showed him his essay and outlined the case against the slave trade. From this time forward Wilberforce was to be the public protagonist of the great cause, in the House of Commons and in the country at large. Clarkson would be the back-stage dynamo, enlisting and organizing support, setting up committees and collecting all the evidence – facts and figures, artifacts and documents and eye-witnesses – that would ultimately make their case unanswerable.

Clarkson travelled all over England, 35,000 miles altogether, at a time when travel was slow and rough and uncomfortable. He interviewed scores of people involved in the slave trade at all levels. He talked his way on to the ships and measured the deck-space available for the negroes and calculated that it came to three square feet per human being for a voyage that would last several weeks, often in stormy conditions. He examined the death rolls, for slaves and for the British seamen, and both were shocking. He gathered the nasty tools of the trade – handcuffs and leg irons – metal instruments to force open the mouths of those who refused to eat, thumb screws. He found a few men who had worked on the ships and were prepared to state publicly what they had witnessed.

His chief ports of call were London and Bristol, Liverpool and Lancaster, and the slave traders soon knew what he was up to. Much of his investigative work took him, naturally, to the harbour areas and public houses. The work became increasingly dangerous, so he took care always to be accompanied by a bodyguard, a powerfully-built young man who carried a pistol in his pocket. Clarkson was frequently engaged in violent arguments, and once, in Liverpool, a gang of thugs tried to throw him off the pier-head into a raging sea.

Clarkson was not a man to be deterred, however. He persisted year after year, preaching the cause in towns and cities, setting up local committees, gathering evidence which he would present to the Prime Minister, William Pitt the Younger, on his return to London. Pitt was personally convinced, but he had only a slender majority in the Commons and he knew that many members of his Tory party had vested interests in the infamous trade. So, although he spoke out forcefully for abolition, he dared not make it a party issue.

Predictably, the slavers closed ranks and brought out the arguments that vested interests traditionally employ to protect their profits: the trade was a vital part of British shipping and mercantile prosperity. If it were abolished we would no longer "rule the waves." Anyway the slaves were not ill treated on the voyages, and many of them found happier lives on the plantations of the New World than they had known in Africa. And even if Britain did renounce the trade, the evil would not be ended because others would move in, particularly the French, our natural rivals and enemies.

When these arguments were disproved, they switched to delaying tactics. There were countless inquiries and debates, and time and again the abolition cause found itself frustrated. Finally, in the winter of 1793-4, Clarkson's health broke down completely under the strain of years of intensive work and repeated disappointment. He had to retire from the fray for many years.

Wilberforce's love for the Lake District might have come into play at this stage. "To live in such a country," he said in a letter, "seems almost like a continual Turtle feast." Clarkson, needing rest and a complete change, went north to stay with an old friend, Thomas Wilkinson, who ran a farm at Yanwath, near Penrith. He helped on the farm, loved it and began to feel better immediately. He paid Wilkinson 1,000 guineas for a 35-acre property at Pooley Bridge at the northern end of Ullswater, and built himself a plain solid house of roughcast stone which commanded tremendous views across the lake to the Hellvelyn range. The house Eusemere, is still there, though it has been greatly enlarged in subsequent years.

Clarkson then made another wise decision. In May 1795 he proposed to a young woman called Catherine, who was good-looking, vivacious, cheerful and witty, widely-read and universally liked. They married and in spring 1796 set off to live in the Lake District. Soon after a child was born and they named him Thomas.

Clarkson was very happy but it was not in his nature to take things easy. "I cannot endure an ideal life," he once said. So he hurled himself into farming – wheat, oats, turnips, sheep, bullocks – and wrote several books: a *Portrait of Quakerism,* a memoir of William Penn, and a massive history of the campaign against the slave trade.

He was an early admirer of Wordsworth's poetry, and soon after William and Dorothy Wordsworth had settled into Dove Cottage, Grasmere, the Clarksons called on them.

"Mr and Mrs Clarkson came to dinner," Dorothy said in a letter, "and stayed with us till after dinner on Monday. Mr Clarkson is the man who took so much pains about the slave trade... Mrs C. is a pleasant woman. We are going there (to Eusemere) next Wednesday and shall probably stay till the Sunday after. We intend walking over the mountains and Mr and Mrs Clarkson will meet us with a boat at Patterdale."

It was the beginning of a close and long-lasting friendship. The two men enjoyed each other's company. Both were grave and intelligent, interested in current affairs; both preferred country life to that in the city. The great attachment, though, was that between the two women. Dorothy adored and admired her brother but she badly needed more entertaining and light-hearted

189

company, someone – like Catherine Clarkson – who was sensible but also bright and funny, interested in all the local gossip and stories. They took to each other immediately and immensely, exchanging letters, visits and intimacies. Mrs Clarkson was one of the very few, outside the Wordsworth family, who was told about William's youthful love affair in France and the daughter he had there. Even Coleridge, Wordsworth's closest friend was not told about that.

It was after a few days visit to Eusemere in April 1802 that Dorothy and William set off on the long walk home to Grasmere on a wild and windy morning, and came across a vision that has become part of English literature. She described it in her Journal... "When we were in the woods beyond Gowbarrow Park we saw a few daffodils close to the water side. We fancied that the lake had floated the seeds ashore and that the little colony had so sprung up. But as we went along there were more and yet more and at last under the boughs of the trees, we saw that there was a long belt of them along the shore, about the breadth of a country turnpike road. I never saw daffodils so beautiful – they grew among the mossy stones about and about them, some rested their heads upon these stones as on a pillow for weariness and the rest tossed and reeled and danced and seemed as if they verily laughed with the wind that blew upon them over the lake, they looked so gay ever glancing ever changing."

It has become the most famous passage in Dorothy's incomparable Journal, because it was reading it some two years after the event that inspired Wordworth to compose the little poem for which he is now (alas!) chiefly remembered.

The Clarksons left the Lake District in 1803 but their friendship with the Wordsworths continued, sustained by regular letters and occasional visits for many years more. Dorothy's liveliest letters are those she wrote to Catherine, whom she always addressed as "my very dear friend."

Back in the south, Clarkson threw himself into the old struggle with all his old enthusiasm. He made further punishing tours, fact-finding and drumming up support, and he was there in March 1807 when the Bill abolishing the slave trade finally passed into law.

Wordsworth wrote an undistinguished sonnet of congratulation, opening with the line: "Clarkson, it was an obstinate hill to climb…"

Coleridge described him as a "moral steam engine" and "The Giant with one Idea," and praised him as "a benefactor of mankind; and this from the purest motives. He, if ever human being did it, listened exclusively to his conscience, and obeyed its voice."

Clarkson went on fighting the good fight. In 1818 he spoke long and earnestly to the Czar of Russia, striving (unsuccessfully) to persuade him to use his influence with the European rulers to get them to suppress the slave trade in their territories. He fought for the abolition of slavery in Britain's West Indian island possessions. He worked, too, to advise and encourage the anti-slavery movement in the United States. He was made a freeman of the City of London in 1839, and died in 1846. His widow outlived him by a further 10 years.

Dorothy Wordsworth

No sister ever gave more loving and devoted service to her brother than Dorothy Wordsworth gave to her brother William. She adored him from infancy and recognized long before anybody else, except for William himself, of course, that he was a genius, a special spirit, dedicated to poetry. And no sister was ever thanked so much and so marvellously:

> … Mine eyes did ne'er
> Fix on a lovely object, nor my mind

Above: The kitchen at Dove Cottage

Take pleasure in the midst of happy thoughts,
But either she, whom now I have, who now
Divides with me this loved abode, was there,
Or not far off. Where'er my footsteps turned,
Her voice was like a hidden Bird that sang;
The thought of her was like a flash of light
Or an unseen companionship, a breath
Of fragrance independent of the wind...

Time and again, in the full flow of his verse, he would pause to express his gratitude to her. Others gave her high praise too. Coleridge, when he first met her, wrote of "Wordsworth's exquisite sister." De Quincey, who met her several years later, portrayed her in ever more ecstatic style. It is not that she was conventionally beautiful or even good looking. But she was very striking: "I may sum up in one brief abstract the sum total of Miss Wordsworth's character, as a companion, by saying that she was the very wildest (in the sense of the most natural) person I have ever known; and also the truest, most inevitable, and at the same time the quickest and readiest in her sympathy, with either joy or sorrow, with laughter or with tears, with the realities of life or the larger realities of the poets!"

De Quincey's is the most lively and brilliant portrait of her – for several years he was virtually one of the family – but others who knew her well in the years of her young womanhood give the same picture, the opposite (almost) of the conventional Jane Austenish young lady of the period. Her complexion was gypsy-like, "Egyptian brown," because she was out in the open air as often as possible. She was short and slight in figure, quick and vivid in manner, alive with sympathies and perceptions and feelings. Open and impulsive.

The words that recur again and again in descriptions of her

Dorothy Wordsworth in old age

are "ardent" and "natural." It is not surprising that she shocked many of her stuffier, more "bourgeois" relations; nor is it surprising that she enchanted many others. Several young men, including William Hazlitt, proposed to her, but her devotion to

William was too strong for her to say yes.

William was the elder by some 20 months and they were friends from the beginning, playing together along the banks of the River Derwent behind their handsome town house in Cockermouth. But when Dorothy was only six their mother died and the family was split up. William went to school in Hawkeshead, then to Cambridge, then on travels in France and Britain. Dorothy moved between relatives, in Penrith and Halifax and elsewhere, some of whom she liked and some she could not stand. She kept in touch with William by letters and occasional brief encounters, but it was not until she was in her early twenties that she was reunited with William on a long holiday in Keswick, when they rediscovered the joys of each other's company and the delights of fell walking. From this time on there was no doubt in either mind that they would spend their lives together. A few years later they found Dove Cottage in Grasmere and moved in, at Christmas 1799, and launched into the three most marvellous years of her life. It is beautifully recorded in the journal she kept, her modest masterpiece.

She started it in May 1800 when William left on a journey, and noted in the first entry: "...I set about keeping my resolve because I will not quarrel with myself, and because I shall give Wm Pleasure by it when he comes home again."

It is a daily, unpretentious account of her housework and her walks, her chats with neighbours and passing beggars, her observations and thoughts, her longing for letters when William is away, his writing when he is at home, their reading and their growing concern about Coleridge, his declining health and collapsing marriage, the garden and the weather and the seasons and the birds. There is disappointingly little of their conversation, of Wordsworth's thoughts or methods of work, or his discussions with Coleridge. But what is left is made unique and radiant by the clean, simple, totally truthful style and its frequent flashes of vision and sensitivity.

She tried her hand at poetry and soon realized that she did not have the knack. But there were many times too, she knew, when the light and the landscape made her "more than half a poet." Again and again, aiming only for the truth and never for literary effect, she strikes exactly the right note and brings the scene or the feeling to vivid light:

"A very fine moonlight night – The moon shone like herrings in the water."

"As we were going along we were stopped at once, at the distance perhaps of 50 yards from our favourite Birch tree. It was yielding to the gusty wind with all its tender twigs, the sun shone upon it and it glanced in the wind like a flying sunshiny shower. It was a tree in shape with stem and branches but it was like a spirit of water."

"We overtook old Fleming at Rydale, leading his little Dutchman-like grandchild along the slippery road. The same pace seemed to be natural to them both, the old man and the little child, and they went hand in hand, the grandfather cautious, yet looking proud of his charge."

"William wasted his mind in the magazines."

"There we lay, ate our dinner and stayed there till about 4 o'clock or later. William and Coleridge repeated and read verses. I drank a little Brandy and water and was in Heaven."

"I went through the fields and sat half an hour, afraid to pass a Cow. The Cow looked at me and I looked at the Cow, and whenever I stirred the Cow gave over eating."

Her most famous passage is that in which she describes the "long belt" of daffodils dancing along the shores of Ullswater that April morning in 1802 when she and William passed that way, which moved him, two years later when he was glancing through the journal, to write the poem by which he is now chiefly remembered. But many more of his poems, and some better ones than Daffodils, were inspired by Dorothy's jottings. A number of his reflective verses, like Resolution and Independence, were inspired by talks with old labourers on the roadsides. It was not William who had these chats. He was a singularly private man. It was Dorothy who talked and gossiped and got people's stories off them, then noted them down in the journal. Later William would read them, and the idea would start to blossom.

This magical period of her life came to an end in January 1803, soon after William married. Dorothy knew Mary Hutchinson well and liked her greatly, and they settled down to an unusually successful ménage a trois. But between the lines of the journal you can discern the profound distress of Dorothy when it became clear that she was no longer to have her brother solely to herself. From now on he had to be shared – with his wife and then with the five children – and though it remained a very happy household, things would never be the same again.

She carried on writing but from now on it was letters. William did not like letter-writing and avoided it as much as he could, but Dorothy enjoyed it. She liked a good gossip, and could be entertaining and informative and fiercely censorious. Mrs Colcridge is dismissed as "a sad fiddle-faddler," for example, and the literary critic, Francis Jeffrey, who persisted in deriding Wordsworth's poetry, as "that ignorant coxcomb."

She remained an integral and vital part of the family through good years and bad – the death of their beloved sailor brother John, the death in 1812 of two of the children – the moves to Allan Bank and the Grasmere Rectory and finally to the grand house at Rydal Mount. Dorothy was very concerned that her friend Catherine Clarkson might think they were "setting up for fine folks" because they had bought themselves "a Turkey carpet," the first carpet they had ever owned. Increased prosperity came with the years, Wordsworth's poetry began to receive widespread recognition at last, the surviving children grew up, and Dorothy remained active and busy, gardening and walking and copying out the new poems as they flowed from his mind. It all came to an end when she was nearly 60. Her health suddenly collapsed. She developed violent disorders of the bowels, took to laudanum to attempt a cure, but grew so weak and listless that she was scarcely able to go out of doors.

For the rest of her long life – she outlived her brother by five years – she was little more than a vegetable, a terrible contrast to the ardent, alert, observant and enthusiastic woman of the past. It was her brother's turn now to repay the years of devotion and inspiration she had given, and he did not fail her. He looked after her carefully, never forgetting the years when he had been poor and unrecognized and his sister had been his eyes and ears:

> A heart, the fountain of sweet tears;
> And love, and thought and joy.

George Macauley Trevelyan

When you consider this north-western corner of England and its rich web of literary associations, you think primarily and quite properly of the poets, Wordsworth, Coleridge, Southey, Tennyson and Norman Nicholson. There are novelists too, Hugh Walpole, Melvyn Bragg and others; childrens' writers like Beatrix Potter and Arthur Ransome; assorted prophets and critics and essayists and journalists, among them John Ruskin and De Quincey and Harriet Martineau. One major area of writing that seems to be missing is history and biography. There was W.G. Collingwood, of course, but he was a local rather than a national

Above: Trevelyan's house at Robin Ghyll.

historian and in some ways more of an antiquarian than an historian. There have been other writers of local history. But for a long time I could think of no leading national historian who had done at least some of his work in Cumbria.

I was wrong.

There was indeed such a man, as I found out when a friend suggested I go to the Langdale Valley and search for a house called Robin Ghyll and look into its history. I found the house just beyond Chapel Style, an old, low, stone

George Macaulay Trevelyan

building with a porch and an acre or so of rough garden, perched modestly on the steep fellside above the road. It belongs to the National Trust who rent it to Tom Wilson, a potter who specializes in miniatures, and his wife Elizabeth. Before they moved in, just over ten years ago, it was used as a climbers' hut. Mrs. Wilson told me that they had found it in a dilapidated state, extremely cold and draughty everywhere, everything a mess, graffiti on the walls. Over ten years they have transformed it into a cosy and comfortable home, with all mod cons and without any way disturbing the feeling of an old Cumberland homestead. It was built in 1702 by a man called Anthony Harrison. Originally it was called Harrison Place. Mrs. Wilson, who is interested in the history of the house found a legal document dated 1704, which shows Harrison buying land at Ellers further up the valley.

Exactly two centuries later, in 1904 – by which time it had the name Robin Ghyll, the house was acquired by Miss Dorothy Ward, a daughter of the highly successful novelist Mrs. Humphrey Ward (who was a grand-daughter of Dr Arnold of Rugby School and who had grown up at Fox How, the doctor's home at Rydal). Dorothy Ward used the place as a holiday home for herself and members of the family. Among those who made full use of it were her sister Janet and her husband, a young Cambridge don who was keen on fell walking and fell running and whose name was George Macaulay Trevelyan.

Trevelyan was born to be a historian. He was a great-nephew of Lord Macaulay, the leading Victorian historian, and named in his honour. His father, George Otto Trevelyan, was a statesman and an impressive historian. Before he was ten years old the young George Macaulay Trevelyan was listening, enthralled, as his mother read aloud from the famous third chapter of his great-uncle's History of England. It was no wonder, then that the boy went on to study history at Trinity College, Cambridge.

By 1904 he was teaching it at the same college. He had already had one book published and was soon to begin work on a three-volume account of Garibaldi's fight for Italian independence. Later on, after distinguished service in the First World War, Trevelyan was to make himself the best-known English historian of the period – with his own History of England, later with English Social History. He was a historian of the old school, not driven by political or sociological dogmas but trying to recreate the past exactly as it must have felt like at the time.

"Disinterested intellectual curiosity," he said, "is the life blood of real civilization." He became a grand and rather forbidding figure, Master of Trinity and virtual Historian-Laureate. It was he who wrote King George the Fifth's jubilee speech to the Houses of Parliament in 1935.

Trevelyan had loved the Lake District since his student days, when he went to Seatoller in Borrowdale on reading parties. He and his friends would study each morning, then go out to explore the fells in the afternoons. He was a fast and almost tireless hill walker, and no-one could match his speed in the descent of steep, rough ground. He believed his ankles were unbreakable. It was he together with his close friend, the mountaineer Geoffrey Winthrop Young who founded the four-day man hunt across the fells, which began at Whitsun 1898 and which still takes place each year.

He was in the first year of his marriage when his sister-in-law, Dorothy Ward, got Robin Ghyll. Within a few months she had made the house habitable, and in June 1905, Trevelyan and his wife and their four-month-old daughter Mary spent the first of many holidays there. They loved everything about it, the primitive, simple living conditions, the freshness of the air, the freedom of the fells, their superb views across the wide valley floor to Crinkle Crags and Bowfell and the Langdale Pikes.

Trevelyan found it conducive to his writing, too. He wrote to his sister-in-law: "I have lived in the mountains by sitting on this glorious terrace for the last ten days. I never got through so much work and at the same time kept so fit, and I believe it is largely due to the place, which is not a hole as most Lake dwellings are."

The baby daughter grew up to be a distinguished writer herself. Under her married name, Mary Moorman, she published a marvellous two-volume biography of Wordsworth. She also wrote a Memoir of her father, in which she recalled their holidays in Langdale. "It was a perfect place for George to work in; much of the Garibaldi trilogy was written there, in the dark little dining room which he used as his study. Every now and then of course he pushed off to the hills for one of his tremendous walks. He bathed every morning in a pool in the ghyll which ran down the fellside close to the house, and he also had a wooden seat made under the very ancient yew tree behind the house whence he could look out at will over the valley."

The Yew tree is still there, at the top of the steep slope behind the house, but the wooden seat has gone.

After that first holiday, the Trevelyans went year after year to Langdale for long summer breaks. Mary Moorman's account makes it clear that, if the amenities were Spartan, they did not lack for domestic help: "It had no bathroom or water sanitation until about 1925 and was therefore the abode of very simple comforts, and I am sure it was not as beloved by the domestic staff (consisting of our cook, a house-parourmaid and nannies, as it was by us."

Many eminent friends went to stay with them – Mrs. Humphrey Ward of course, Geoffrey Winthrop Young, Virginia Woolf, Canon Rawnsley from Keswick, Julian Huxley the biologist. Just before the outbreak of the First World War, Bruno Garibaldi, grand-son of the Italian hero, was their guest there.

In 1906 a son, Theodore, was born, and soon after the Trevelyans had a wooden nursery built on the back of the house so that the children would have somewhere to play in wet weather. The extension was stoutly built. Today, 80 years on or so, Tom Wilson uses the nursery as a workshop. You can still see the old black-boards, and the wooden walls still keep the weather out and the warmth in.

When the weather was fine their father would take the children out on to the rough fellside above the house and organize exciting "Robin Hood" games with bows and arrows. From their vantage point above the vale they could watch coach-loads of tourists passing along the road in their horse-drawn vehicles, and climbers, festooned with hemp ropes, walking to the crags. Some days their mother hired a pony and trap and they would go off to spend the day, picnicking and exploring a neighbouring valley. They often called, on the way home, to take tea with "Aunt Fran" at Fox How, the last surviving child of Dr. Arnold.

In 1911 Trevelyan bought Robin Ghyll from his sister-in-law for £200. That same year brought a terrible tragedy. On a spring holiday in Dorset, Theodore, five years old, died suddenly of appendicitis. It is a measure of the depth of their attachment to Langdale that, although the family home was in London, they took the boy's body to the church in the valley for burial. Trevelyan wrote to a friend: "Now my bravest hopes lie buried here in the fellside graveyard, beneath the bracken and the rocks, and this is the place of my heart."

The family were at Robin Ghyll in August 1914 when the war began. Julian Huxley was staying with them and, many years later, writing his "Memories," he remembered the breakfast table on the fateful morning and Trevelyan in tears and saying: "It will be war, and millions of human beings are going to be killed in this senseless business." He was a better prophet than most of his countrymen, who were confident that it would all be over by Christmas. They were still in Langdale at the end of the month, when Trevelyan was amused by a completely baseless rumour that swept through the Lake District.

"People round here," he said in a letter, "believe firmly that

Lord Lonsdale has been arrested for treasonable correspondence with the Kaiser." The German Emperor, Kaiser Wilhelm, by this time the most hated man in England, had been a pre-war friend of the Earl's and more than once had been his guest for the grouse-shooting on the Lowther estates.

For the greater part of the war Trevelyan was in the mountains of northern Italy, commanding an ambulance unit with efficiency and gallantry. When he felt homesick, as he often did, it was for Robin Ghyll and the Lakeland fells. After the war the Langdale holidays were resumed and his career blossomed.

His books, especially the History of England, made him famous and comparatively wealthy. In 1927 he was made Regius Professor of Modern History at Cambridge.

He had become increasingly concerned over the growing threats to the Lake District landscape from tourism and from insensitive exploitation. He used his new-found wealth to buy three farms at the head of Langdale, Stool End, Wall End and Dungeon Ghyll, and presented them to the National Trust. It is a significant moment in Lake District history because this marked the beginning of a new line of policy by the National Trust. Previously, when they had acquired land and property, they had opened them to the public.

Now, they inaugurated the system by which the farms were rented out, with the Trust keeping control over the way they were managed to make sure nothing was done to harm the character of the region.

Throughout the 1930's, in the midst of a busy working life, Trevelyan found time and energy to fight for the Lake District. He bought more farms in Langdale, and some at the head of Buttermere too, and covenanted them to the National Trust. He was an enthusiastic President of the Youth Hostels Association, eager that more and more young people should discover the delights he had found in exploring the country. When it became public knowledge that the Forestry Commission was planning to cover much of Eskdale and the Duddon Valley with a blanket of conifers, he hurled himself into the fray, organizing the opposition, writing to "The Times," recruiting the support of his many influential friends. He wrote a booklet called "Must England's Beauty Perish?" He earned himself a place in the noble dynasty of those like Canon Rawnsley, Beatrix Potter, the Rev. H.H. Symonds, who defended the district from the predators in the years before it became a national park.

When his wife died in 1956, she was buried in Langdale Churchyard. Six years later, when Trevelyan died, he too was buried there. On the wall of the barn of Side House Farm in upper Langdale, a mile beyond Robin Ghyll, there is an inscribed green slate. It was dedicated to the memory of George Macaulay Trevelyan in 1965. Its message states simply and truly, that he loved Langdale "above all other places."

Wicked Jimmy: The Earl of Lonsdale

This is the story of two remarkable men and the strained relationship that developed between them. It reflects no credit on either of them – or anyone else, for that matter.

One of them was James Boswell, Laird of Auchinleck in Ayrshire, friend and biographer of Dr Samuel Johnson, lawyer and lecher and a great deal else besides. He will be read and enjoyed for as long as anyone can read – for the great biography and also for the astonishingly frank Journals which he kept for most of his life and which shocked the world when they were finally published some two centuries after being written.

In the other corner, a man who could hardly have been more contrasting – Sir James Lowther, Earl of Lonsdale, the richest and most powerful man in North West England in the second half of the 18th Century. He was also one of the most obnoxious men who ever lived. His inherited wealth derived from the coal and iron ore of the Cumberland coastline, and he used it to extend his political influence. He had complete control over nine seats in the House of Commons. He was selfish and greedy, uncouth in manner and unscrupulous in methods, overbearing and litigious, moody and mean-spirited, an aristocratic lout of the first degree. James Lowther was so outstandingly unpleasant that, in an age when men of position were expected to show scant regard for others, he was widely despised.

His universal nickname was "Wicked Jimmy."

"Wicked Jimmy"

These two disparate figures came together at the close of 1787.

The reason was simple. Boswell needed to enhance his career. He had been a lawyer for years but had consistently neglected professional work, preferring the pleasures of travel, the society of men of wit and culture, and the pursuit of women of all kinds. Now, however, he was approaching 50, a married man with five small children. The chief distraction of his earlier life, Dr Johnson, was dead. Boswell was writing the biography, it was nearing completion, but he had serious need of a position and a regular income. In 18th Century England this meant he needed a patron.

In his *Dictionary of the English Language,* Dr Johnson had used the word patron to deliver one of his opinionated definitions: "One who countenances, supports or protects. Commonly a wretch who supports with insolence, and is paid with flattery." Even more famously, in his letter to Lord Chesterfield, his own so-called patron, Johnson had written: "Is not a patron, my Lord, one who looks with unconcern on a man struggling for life in the water and when he has reached the ground, encumbers him with help?"

Boswell was aware of Dr Johnson's feelings on the subject; he knew how unhelpful Chesterfield had been to Johnson when the help was really needed. But he felt he had no alternative. He wanted a new law job, and he wanted it, if possible, near to his family seat at Auchinleck. Inexorably, this pointed to Sir James Lowther. Boswell approached the great man, hoping to win his favour and become Recorder of Carlisle, which might in turn lead to a seat in the House of Commons as one of "Lowther's ninepins."

Boswell called on Sir James, at his London house, on December 1787. He was graciously received and according to his Journal, given a promise that the Recordership would be his. Sir James said he was setting off for Cumberland next morning, and would Boswell go with him? Boswell could hardly believe his luck. He packed in a hurry and was back at the house at 9 next morning. There was a long delay before Sir James was ready to set off but Boswell, full of hope, endured it patiently, and felt very grand indeed as His Lordship's carriage bowled northwards, and joined Sir James in the singing of several songs from *The Beggar's Opera.*

The journey to Lowther took two days and Boswell began to see something of his patron in action. He was shocked: "He damned and scolded about bad beef, etc., and was irritated that a bolt of the coach was broke and had to be mended, which took some time. Two shillings were charged. He would give only one; and because the Wetherby boys had not come in less than an hour and 20 minutes he gave them only sixpence apiece and nothing to the ostler... His way was to call: 'Boys, I'm in a great hurry. Make haste or I'll give you nothing. I'm not to waste my lungs calling to you. I have looked at my watch. If I have to call you again you shall have nothing. If I must waste my lungs I must save my cash.'"

They reached Lowther Castle on the evening of December 23rd and there was no welcome there, nothing but warm milk to see them off to bed: "Dreadfully cold in the waste dining-room, and there was a railing of iron painted green to keep us off the hearth that it might be clean. In this whim He was obstinate. Bedroom cold, cold."

It was the bad start to a thoroughly bleak, uncomfortable and apparently endless stay, days of frustration and humiliation for Boswell. It was probably the low-point of his whole life.

Sir James' method was manic. He could turn on the charm and give the impression that he was only too eager to give friendly assistance. More often though, he was surly and discouraging. It was all governed entirely, by his own whim of the moment. He liked to keep his dependents dependent, and worried.

Boswell had been the guest of many greater men – among

them Voltaire and Rousseau and the Corsican freedom-fighter Pasquale Paoli – and none of them had treated him with such brutal and arbitrary lack of consideration. Sir James' henchmen assured Boswell that there was nothing personal in it: Sir James treated everybody like that. But it fell particularly hard on Boswell, because he was used to dealing with eminent men on an equal basis, and thought of himself as a man of freedom and independent spirit. After all, the world knew him as "Corsica Boswell," the leading British protagonist for the freedom of that island from foreign rule.

It is an impressive measure of his need that he controlled his feelings, and held his tongue for so long.

"I was quite dull and dispirited and gloomy," he wrote in the Journal, "for we all sat in vile, timid restraint." Later in the same day he noted: "While Lonsdale was drowsy after dinner, we sat in stupid silence, and I groaned inwardly. I could not help showing impatience at this treatment. I turned myself some time restlessly upon my chair and then went up to my room, where I meditated sullenly what I should do, sometimes thinking of setting off on foot for Clifton, a village two miles off through which the mail-coach comes, and from thence getting off for London this very night, sometimes of going to bed."

He hardly slept that night, turning his problems over in his mind, resolving to take a firm line, then deciding to further extend his patience. He was missing his family, and anxious about his wife's health. He ruminated upon Sir James' character: "… this painful discovery of his being the worst man in the world for a patron … I saw in Him that vast wealth and influence do not produce proportionate happiness…"

He lay in till after 10 next morning, then got up, packed his travelling-bag and crept out of the house undetected. There was snow on the ground – Sir James had used this as his excuse for delaying a trip to Whitehaven Castle – but Boswell got as far as Penrith, then changed his mind and walked back again. He was determined to confront Sir James and this he now did, stating that he had to be back in London by January 6th at the latest, and that he no longer wanted the Recordership. At this Sir James came over all concerned, and insisted that the job was his for the asking. Once again, Boswell's heart filled with hope and confidence that his career was assured: "This conversation gave quite a new turn to my spirits... The relief of the Recordership, the little comforts of the stomach, and the prospect of moving next day to Whitehaven Castle, which I was assured was warm, made me go to bed in tranquility. Such is the human mind."

Such, indeed, was Boswell's mind.

They went to Whitehaven the next day, December 29th, Boswell delighted that "for the first time in my life I was driven in a coach and six." The roads had been cleared for them, snow piled high at the sides: "We drove to Keswick, where we had six fresh horses," Boswell noted. "I could scarcely distinguish two of the lakes from the surrounding snow. But Saddleback and other mountains and the famed Skiddaw looked sublime."

Despite the snow, they went over Whinlatter Pass, then by way of Cockermouth to Whitehaven Castle, which – to Boswell's relief – was warm and elegant and spacious. Even so they were given a poor dinner and not enough to drink. Sir James was being curmudgeonly again.

Now Boswell had to endure more long days of inaction and uncertainty, with plenty of bad behaviour from his patron and plenty of bad weather outside. He was taken to admire the harbour in pouring rain, and two days later Sir James showed him round a timber-yard: "His slow progress and insensibility to rain fretted me."

Boswell was also beginning to fret again about the Recordership and also about his wife's health; she had consumption. January 6th, the day he said he must be back in London, found him still at Whitehaven Castle, and the same day brought a letter saying his wife was "not at all well." He again confronted Sir James, "whose indifference as to my tranquillity was shocking."

When Boswell asked about the Recordership, the reply he got was "We shall see."

In fact, it was already fixed. Boswell was at last allowed to leave for Carlisle on January 10th. He entertained the mayor to supper that night, and next morning the aldermen gathered at the Moot Hall and the vote went conclusively in Boswell's favour. The job was his. He made a speech, then took everyone who had voted for him off for a drunken celebration.

Boswell was back home in London on January 14th, much relieved to find his wife considerably recovered. But her improvement was only temporary. She died six months later.

In the months that followed Boswell got some revenge on Sir James by neglecting his duties in Carlisle as much as he dared. Sir James countered by making it clear Boswell had no hope of getting one of his pocket-borough seats in Parliament. He actually told Boswell it would not be a good thing because he would only "get drunk and make a foolish speech."

In mid-June 1790 Sir James insisted that Boswell should go with him to Carlisle to supervise the coming elections. It was vastly inconvenient for Boswell at that moment because his *Life of Samuel Johnson* was going through the printers. He was made to go, nonetheless, and as soon as the journey began there was serious trouble.

Boswell, probably out of angry resentment at being there at all, started bragging about his "liberal and independent views."

Sir James cut in sharply: "You have kept low company all your life. What are you, Sir?"

Boswell responded: "A man of honour, and I hope to show myself such."

To which Sir James replied: "You will be settled when you have a bullet in your belly."

This was duelling talk. When they stopped at Barnet for the night, Boswell left the inn to see if there were any army officers in the town, prepared to lend him a pair of pistols. Mercifully he found none, and as the two men sat over their cold dinner they patched up the quarrel. Neither of them had been looking forward to a duel.

So they proceeded to Carlisle, where Boswell did what was required of him. Then he wrote his resignation. In a letter to a close friend he said: "I parted from the Northern Tyrant in a strange equivocal state, for he was half irritated, half reconciled." He also said that he had sworn henceforth to be quite independent of Sir James. That was a promise he managed to keep.

The great work, the *Life of Samuel Johnson,* was published in May 1791, to almost universal acclaim. Boswell died four years later, never having secured the steady, lucrative post he had longed for.

Sir James Lowther lived on until May 1802, not mellowing with age in any detectable way. To the very end he refused to pay the debt he had owed to the Wordsworth family of Cockermouth for 19 years.

John Wordsworth, father of William and Dorothy and three other children, had died at Christmas 1783. For many years he had worked as a legal agent for Sir James, and when he died Sir

James owed him some £4,700, a very considerable amount in those days. It would certainly have made a great difference to the lives of the Wordsworth children. But Sir James would not pay, preferring to use his wealth and influence to confuse the courts and delay any settlement.

It was not until his death, and the succession to the Lowther fortune of a much more decent and honourable man, that the debt, plus the accrued interest, was paid.

Wordsworth

Over the last couple of years I have written a dozen articles in this series about writers and the places in Cumbria where they lived and worked, and it seems little short of miraculous – some might say reprehensible – that I should have got so far without dealing with the most important of them all.

To most people the names William Wordsworth and the Lake District are all but synonymous. He has many mentions in my previous articles, of course, because he was the friend or acquaintance or mentor or inspiration to most of the people I have written about. Several of them – like Coleridge and De Quincey and Dr Arnold of Rugby – came to live in the Lake District

Above: Rydal Mount

simply because it was Wordsworth country.

There is no getting away from the man. His is the dominating *Genius Locii,* the all-pervading spirit of the place. He did not, as some people seem to think, actually invent the district. He was not even the first fine writer to sing its praises. But he knew the area better, more widely and more deeply, than anyone else (at least until Norman Nicholson came along a century later), and he portrayed the mountain landscape and what it meant to him with unparalleled

William Wordsworth

power and penetration. There are phrases and passages in the great poems – *Tintern Abbey* and *Intimations of Immortality* and the first books of *The Prelude* –that lodge themselves in the mind and reverberate there and never lose their thrilling force. More than any other writer in English it was Wordsworth who conditioned the way in which we now look at nature and the wilderness. It was he who first prophetically suggested that the district should be made "a sort of National property, in which every man has a right and interest who has an eye to perceive and a heart to enjoy."

And more than any other writer in this series – once again the only comparable figure is Norman Nicholson – Wordsworth was a complete Cumbrian. He was born in Cockermouth and passed the first part of his life on the northern edge of the Lake District, within sight of Skiddaw. Then he was sent to school at

Hawkeshead, to spend blissful and formative years among the gentler hills of the southern part of the district. After a period of travel and uncertainty – moving about between Cambridge, London, Wales, France, South-West England and Germany – he returned to his native heath to make a home for himself and his family in the very heart of the fells, at Grasmere and Rydal. There he spent the last 50 years of his life, walking vigorously in all directions, writing continuously in prose as well as poetry, welcoming friends and showing them round, growing old and famous, a great national guru. Wordsworth lived a long and highly creative life. He is so outstanding, so intimately connected to so many different parts of Cumbria, and his life is so richly documented – in his own writings as well as in the journals and letters and reminiscences of many friends and relations – that he positively demands at least two articles instead of the usual one.

The demand can clearly be heard nearly a century and a half after his death. He was not a man to raise his voice but he could be compellingly firm.

He shall have two articles.

He was born in April 1770 in the large, handsome house on Cockermouth's Main Street, which is now known simply as Wordsworth House. Pevsner describes it as "quite a swagger house for such a town: standing on its own, nine windows wide and with moulded window frames and a porch with Tuscan columns." In much of his verse Wordsworth spoke of, and for, the simple very basic life of the peasant. But this is no peasant's home. In fact, it never belonged to the Wordsworth family. It was built in 1745 and very soon, like so much else in Cumberland and Westmorland in those days, became the property of Sir James Lowther, the grasping and widely-hated grandee of the region.

Wordsworth House, Cockermouth

When William's father, John Wordsworth, became law agent to Sir James, he got the use of the house. When John died, the house reverted to Sir James. In the late 1930s it was proposed to raze it to the ground to make a bus station for the town, but this philistine plan was fiercely opposed. A public campaign was successful, and in 1939 the house was handed over to the National Trust to become a memorial to the poet. It is still run by the trust who recently had it painted a rather odd, terra cotta colour on the outside. Inside it is sparse but very elegant, with period furniture and furnishings, a charming portrayal of the domestic interior of the upper middle class in the latter half of the 18th Century. From the other side of the busy main road a bust of Wordsworth gazes across at the home of his childhood.

It was a very happy childhood. The best account, naturally is his own – in the first book of *The Prelude.* He describes himself playing in the walled garden at the back of the house and along the terrace beyond, exploring the banks of the River Derwent, splashing all day long in the mill-race, chasing butterflies, establishing the foundations of his life-long attachment to his sister Dorothy, 21 months his junior. He summed it all up in the memorable lines:

> *Fair seed-time had my soul, and I grew up*
> *Fostered alike by beauty and by fear.*

And in another poem he acknowledged the debt he owed Dorothy:

> *She gave me eyes, she gave me ears,*
> *And humble cares, and delicate fears,*
> *A heart, the fountain of sweet tears,*
> *And love, and thought, and joy.*

It was a lively family of five children, all of whom – remarkably for that time – grew up to adulthood. William was sent to local schools, in Penrith as well as Cockermouth, but his true education was at home where there was a good library. He read fairy stories and novels and the great English poets who were to form the steady basis of his reading throughout his life – Spenser, Shakespeare, Milton.

The father was a busy man and often away from home, but the mother, Ann, was a calm and capable woman, well able to cope without making a fuss. She was shrewd, too. She once said that William "was the only one of her children for whom she felt any anxiety; he had such capacities for good or evil."

Clearly, he was a bright and active boy lively-minded and capable of concentration but he also showed – from the beginning – signs of that steady, resolute will-power that was to be a leading characteristic of the man. "The child is father to the man" (his famous paradox) – certainly applied to him. Even as a child he refused to submit quietly to overbearing authority, which he most often encountered at the home of his mother's parents. He could be rebellious and defiant. In the last years of his life, he recalled: "I was of a stiff, moody and violent temper; so much so that I remember going once into the attic of my grandfather's house at Penrith, upon some indignity having been put upon me, with an intention of destroying myself with one of the foils which I knew was kept there. I took the foil in my hand, but my heart failed."

He was nearly eight years old when this secure family life was shattered by the death of his mother. His father was distracted by grief and survived a few more desolate years by immersing himself in his work. The children were dispersed – Dorothy to live with relatives in Halifax, the boys to the Old Grammar School at Hawkeshead.

The small, simple but delightful Tudor building still stands and William's initials can be seen carved into a desk top. The school had a high reputation. Most English schools at that time were brutal institutions, but the grammar school at Hawkeshead was run on more enlightened, humanitarian lines. The boys were drilled in the classical languages, Latin and Greek, and the teaching was thorough and rigorous, but a succession of distinguished teachers did their best to inspire a love of language and the habit of reading Virgil, Ovid and Homer.

Wordsworth enjoyed the work but also continued to read the great English poets. And he was encouraged to try his hand at composition. There is nothing impressive about his early work. It was imitative and derivative and gave no sign of the immense originality and individuality that was to come. But he was soundly schooled in the techniques of writing, the laws of prosody. He developed an acute ear for rhythms and cadences, a wide vocabulary, and formed the habit of working away at an idea until he had made its expression in verse as smooth and sweet-sounding and apt as possible. It was this training that gave him the technical mastery that is so remarkable a feature of his work. He could excel in all the poetic forms – lyrics and odes, ballads and narrative verse, the iron disciplines of the sonnet and the expansive freedoms of blank verse.

The boys at Hawkeshead were also taught mathematics and science and what was called "natural philosophy," and William was good at these too. But the key lessons, according to his own incomparable testimony, were learnt not in the classroom but on holidays. There seems to have been a generous amount of free time. And he had the good luck to be lodged with a kindly and elderly woman, Ann Tyson, who looked after her charges well enough but did not worry if they stayed out long after darkness and came home weary and muddy. The young Wordsworth used this free time to the utmost. He explored the fells for miles around, gathered nuts, set snares for woodcock, raided ravens' nests for eggs (which he regretted later on), fished in the rivers, rowed or skated on the lakes, listened to the talk of the local folk. Often he was with other, like-spirited boys. Sometimes he wandered alone with his teeming thoughts. He described his adventures in his autobiographical masterpiece, *The Prelude,* and gave a detailed account of his emergent and very special relationship with nature.

He later believed and it became the theme of his greatest poems – that it was these years that created his unique soul.

The Prelude was sub-titled "Growth of a Poet's mind." It is almost as if he found in the natural world around him a substitute for the parents he had lost. There was an element of fear in the relationship, a sense of the enormous powers of nature and its unfathomable mysteries, his own smallness in the presence of creation. But he found great joy as well, a consoling, calming feeling that he was part of creation, a tiny but vital atom in a vast, harmonious whole. It was an exciting time for him:

We ran a boisterous race, the year span round with giddy motion...

But it was formative, too:

...the earth
And common face of Nature spake to me rememberable things.

He believed that nature had lessons to teach – about patience and endurance, acceptance. Those who grew up in the country and worked on the land were, he thought, better and nobler creatures than those imprisoned in towns and cities. These were convictions that formed in his mind a little late. In his late teens and early twenties, Wordsworth was not entirely immune to the pleasures of civic life. When he was 17 he went to study at Cambridge. In fact he took his studies very casually indeed, became something of a dandy for a short time, and even, on one occasion, drank too much. He later partly excused himself from blame on the grounds that he had been drinking the health of Milton.

It is significant, though, that it was during the first summer holidays from Cambridge, when he was visiting his old haunts around Hawkeshead, that he realized that it was his destiny to be a poet. He went to a village dance that lasted into the early hours. Walking home at dawn, he watched a magnificent sunrise and heard the birds singing and felt his heart full to the brim:

...I made no vows, but vows
Were then made for me; bond unknown to me
Was given, that I should be, else sinning greatly
A dedicated Spirit...

There were many years of struggle and frequent disappointment and perhaps occasional doubt to come, from this time onwards he was sustained by a deep inner certainty that he had been chosen to write great poetry. For a painfully long time there were very few who shared this conviction. But he was right.

And in the end the world acknowledged it.

* * *

At the age of 17 William Wordsworth left the Lake District to become a student in Cambridge and apart from brief occasional visits, he was away from his native heath for seven years. A lot happened to him during that time. His university career was wayward. He twice went to France, then in the early throes of the great revolution, and on the second visit fell in love with a French woman and gave her a child, a daughter. When war between England and France loomed, he hurried home to live in London and travel extensively about southern England and across Wales. It was a period of anxiety and uncertainty for him. Already he felt that providence had marked him out to be a poet. But so far he had written nothing of much apparent merit, and he did not see how he would ever be able to make a living out of that precarious calling.

The period was all the more disturbing for him because he was effectively separated from his much-loved sister Dorothy. They came together again, however, in January 1794. Three months later they set off to return to the Lake District. They took a coach to Kendal, got out to walk along the shores of Windermere, then northwards past Rydal and Grasmere, over Dunmail Raise, down the Thirlmere valley and so to Keswick. An old schoolfriend of William's, William Calvert, had offered them free lodging at the end of his farmhouse at Old Windebrowe on the outskirts of Keswick. They accepted joyfully, and never regretted it.

The few months that followed were of vital importance to both of them. They rediscovered the delights of each other's company. They discovered the delights of walking about the fells and valleys. And the problem of William's financial future was, for the time being, solved.

Soon after they had settled in, in April 1794, Dorothy wrote to a friend: "You cannot conceive anything more beautiful than the situation of this house. It stands upon the top of a very steep bank, which rises in a direction very nearly perpendicular from a dashing stream below. From the window of the room where I write I have a prospect of the road winding along the opposite banks of the river, of a part of the lake of Keswick and of the town, and towering above the town a woody steep of very considerable heights, whose summit is a long range of silver rocks..."

When her stuffy aunt in Penrith wrote to question the propriety of her "rambling about the country on foot," Dorothy riposted magnificently: "As you have not sufficiently developed the reasons of your censure I have endeavoured to discover them, and I confess no other possible objections against my continuing here a few weeks longer suggest themselves, except the expense and that you may suppose me to be in an unprotected situation. As to the former of these objections I reply that I drink no tea, that my supper and breakfast are of bread and milk and my dinner chiefly of potatoes from choice. In answer to the second of these suggestions, namely that I may be supposed to be in an exposed situation, I affirm that I consider the character and virtues of my brother as a sufficient protection..."

The rooms where William and Dorothy lodged very happily now form part of the Calvert Trust charity, which gives adventure holidays to disabled people. William Wordsworth stayed longer than intended, to look after his friend's brother Raisley who was seriously ill with tuberculosis. He was an attentive nurse and Raisley, partly in gratitude, partly in recognition of Wordsworth's latent powers, bequeathed him £900 in his will. It was a considerable sum in those days. Raisley died in January 1795. His legacy proved of incalculable value to the world, enabling Wordsworth to give up all thought of having to adopt some profession – the law, the army, the church – and concentrate on the full-time composition of poetry. In his autobiographical poem The Prelude, he paid tribute to Raisley Calvert as one who did:

> By a bequest sufficient for my needs
> Enable me to pause for choice, and walk
> At large and unrestrain'd, nor damp'd too soon
> By mutual cares...

From this time on brother and sister were rarely apart and never for very long. For a while, though, they were once again away from the Lake District – living in Dorset and Somerset, exploring the Quantocks with Coleridge, planning a new vein English poetry. In 1798 their poems were published, anonymously, under the title Lyrical Ballads. The three friends paid a long visit to Germany, Coleridge studying the language and advanced German thought, Wordsworth writing the Lucy lyrics and starting what was to become a life-long work on the poem about his life The Prelude.

They were back in England before the end of 1799 and in November that year William introduced Coleridge to the fell country of Cumberland and Westmorland. In the course of a vigorous walking tour they noticed a small cottage on the edge of Grasmere. It had been a tiny pub, The Dove and Olive Branch, but now it was empty. Within a few weeks William had agreed to rent it at £8 a year. Just before Christmas he and Dorothy moved in.

At first the house was ice cold. One of the chimneys smoked horribly. They had little in the way of furniture but made it comfortable and ready to welcome guests and worked out plans for the garden. "Dorothy is much pleased with the house and appurtenances, the orchard especially," William wrote to Coleridge. "In imagination she has already built a seat with a summer shed on the highest platform in this our little domestic slip of a mountain." Later in the letter, he said: "Rydale is covered with ice, clear as polished steel. I have procured a pair of skates and tomorrow mean to give my body to the wind..."

There are intriguing echoes in that sentence from the version of The Prelude he was writing at that time, describing his boyhood adventures on skates:

...All shod with steel
We hissed along the polished ice in games
Confederate...
...And often times
When we have given our bodies to the wind...

The cottage in Grasmere is now famous across the English-speaking world as Dove Cottage, the thriving centre of an expanding Wordworth industry, with a museum and a bookshop, café and car park, thousands of visitors each year. In the Wordsworths' time it was called Town End. They lived there for just over eight years. It was only a fraction of the poet's life but, by general consensus and with good reason, it is seen as his halcyon period.

He and Dorothy built their own lives there. "our beautiful and quiet home," he called it. They filled it with friends. When you look round the little cottage and its tiny rooms you wonder how they managed, but they did, and very well. Within two years William had married Mary Hutchinson and brought her to Grasmere where they settled into a perfectly contented menage a trois, a very rare thing. And soon after that the children began to arrive. Dorothy recorded the events, and reflected the spirit of these days in her incomparable Journal. Best of all, William's confidence in his poetic destiny was clearly vindicated – he wrote prolifically and more powerfully than ever before. Poems of all kinds poured from his teeming mind, not effortlessly – composition was always a struggle for him, usually ending in headaches and prostration – but marvellously. The world still failed to recognize him, but he and his family and his friends knew, beyond doubt, that this was a great creative period. He was to go on writing poetry for many more decades, but never again would he attain the heights of these years at Dove Cottage.

In a letter written in February 1805 Wordsworth spoke scathingly of a new house being built across the valley:

"Woe to poor Grasmere for ever and ever! A wretched Creature, wretched in name and Nature, of the name of Crump, goaded on by his still more wretched Wife, this same Wretch has at last begun to put his long impending threats in execution; and when you next enter the sweet paradise of Grasmere you will see staring you in the face, upon that beautiful ridge that elbows out into the vale, (behind the church and towering far above its steeple), a temple of abomination, in which are to be enshrined Mr and Mrs Crump. Seriously, this is a great vexation to us, as this House will stare you in the face from every part of the Vale, and entirely destroy its character of simplicity and seclusion."

Allan Bank

Wordsworth invariably opposed almost all change and was undoubtedly exaggerating the effects of the house that Mr Crump, a Liverpool attorney, was building. It was called Allan Bank and three years later the Wordsworths went to live there. Three children had been born to William and Mary by early 1808 and a fourth was on the way, and Dove Cottage was altogether too over-crowded. So the Wordsworths moved to Allan Bank and De Quincey succeeded them, with thousands of books, into Dove Cottage. Dorothy liked the views from the new home; "Wherever we turn there is nothing more beautiful than we see from our windows, while the treasures of Easedale lie as it were at our door," But she constantly remembered the wonderful years at Dove Cottage, especially when things began to go wrong at Allan Bank.

The adults all liked having a room to themselves and plenty

of space, but the house proved damp and cold and all the chimneys smoked so abominably it was virtually impossible to warm the place up. Whenever they tried, everyone choked and everything was made filthy. By the end of their first year Dorothy was describing Allan Bank as "literally not habitable." Even so, the next two Wordsworth children were born there. Coleridge stayed with them for many months, and it seemed longer since he was becoming ever more heavily addicted to opium and alcohol, making himself in Wordsworth's phrase, "an absolute nuisance" about the house. In May 1811 the Wordsworths moved again, this time to the old Rectory, immediately across the road from the squat tower of Grasmere church.

This was an old building that had not been occupied for many years. It was in a state of disrepair and, like Allan Bank, cold and damp and afflicted with recalcitrant chimneys. It is easy to see why Wordsworth developed his high regard for the importance of properly-working chimneys. These domestic problems continuously distracted him from his writing, and they were still desperately short of money. None of them liked the Rectory, and the place became unbearable in 1812 when two children, Catherine and Thomas, died there within a few months of each other. William always believed that the dampness of the house and the sogginess of the ground all round it had caused the deaths. The children were buried in the graveyard, 100 yards from the Rectory front door. In January 1813, a few weeks after the death of Thomas, "the darling of the whole house" Dorothy was writing: "Our present Residence, which is close to the Churchyard and the school which was our darling's Daily pride and pleasure, is become so melancholy that we have resolved to remove from it, and William has taken a house at Rydale which is very pleasantly situated."

Rydal Mount, two miles south of Grasmere, was the family home for the rest of their lives, almost 40 years in William's case. It was by far the handsomest and grandest of their homes, a spacious and solid building, standing in more than four acres of sloping garden, commanding long views of lake and mountain to the south and the west. Its chimneys, built in the Wordsworth-approved Lakeland style, worked well. It was May Day 1813 when they moved in and straight away there was an all-round lightening of spirits. Next day Dorothy wrote: "The weather is delightful and the place a paradise."

Wordsworth did not own the house. All his homes were rented and for Rydal Mount he paid Lady Fleming £35 a year. But money was no longer a pressing problem. Earlier that year Wordsworth had at last secured a government job, Distributor of Stamps for Westmorland. To Dorothy's delight, they could even afford one or two proper carpets: "Oh that you were here," she wrote to her great friend Mrs Clarkson, "We are going to have a Turkey!!! Carpet – in the dining room and a Brussells in William's study." She went on to give an assurance that they were not setting up for fine folks.

This was true. They kept their habits of careful, Spartan living, though in later years the house was occasionally the scene of large dinner parties and even dances. It was an extended family – William and his wife Mary, their three surviving children, with William's sister Dorothy and Mary's sister Sarah as permanent houseguests. And there were frequent visitors – Coleridge's family, Southey's, friends and fans.

Rydal Mount was a haven of domestic harmony and content. William continued to work hard, doing his official duties conscientiously, landscaping the garden, writing verses. And gradually the recognition came. As his poetic powers declined, the world came to see how great he had been. When Southey died in 1843, William was appointed Poet Laureate, though he did not accept until the Prime Minister had assured him that he would not be required to produce appropriate lines for every royal occasion.

William died at Rydal Mount in April 1850, just turned 70 years of age. Dorothy, whose wits had long deserted her, survived him five years. Mary lingered on till 1859.

It is remarkable proof of the stability of Cumbrian society that all the buildings closely connected with Wordswoth's life are still standing, still looking very much as they did in his day. His birthplace in Cockermouth belongs to the National Trust and is open to the public, Hawkeshead Grammar School can also be inspected, though the old farmhouse at Windy Brow, Keswick, can only be viewed from the outside now. Dove Cottage has belonged to the Wordsworth Trust and has been open to the public for 100 years. Allan Bank is another National Trust building – it was bequeathed to them by the redoubtable Canon Rawnsley who spent his final years there – now rented out privately. Grasmere Rectory, quite properly, is the home of the Rector, who says it is no longer damp and dismal – the ground was drained and the building raised some five feet in 1895. Rydal Mount is still a Wordsworth home. The poet's great-great-granddaughter lives in rooms at the back of the house from time to time, but the rest of the house and the fine gardens have been open to visitors for the past 20 years. The bedrooms are simple, the drawing room is magnificent, and these and other rooms are full of furniture and pictures and books and documents relating to the time when it was the lively, happy centre of the great man's life in the years of his fulfillment.